The Politics of Starvation

By Jack Shepherd

With an afterword by Stephen J. Green

CARNEGIE ENDOWMENT FOR INTERNATIONAL PEACE
NEW YORK   WASHINGTON, D.C.

362.5
S548p

© 1975. Carnegie Endowment for International Peace. All rights reserved, including the right to reproduce this book or portions thereof in any form, except for the inclusion of brief quotations in a review. All inquiries should be addressed to the Carnegie Endowment for International Peace, 11 Dupont Circle, N.W., Washington, D.C. 20036 or 345 East 46th Street, New York, New York 10017.

I.S.B.N. 0-87003-002-7

Library of Congress Catalog Card Number: 75-40831
Cover photo by Photri; cover design by Sheila Freeman.
Printed in the United States of America 78-9419

CONTENTS

FOREWORD v
INTRODUCTION viii

CHAPTERS

I	. . . .	1
II	. . . .	9
III	. . . .	13
IV	. . . .	19
V	. . . .	25
VI	. . . .	31
VII	. . . .	37
VIII	. . . .	47
IX	. . . .	53
X	. . . .	59
XI	. . . .	69
XII	. . . .	79

AFTERWORD 87
SELECTED BIBLIOGRAPHY 99

FOREWORD

Any new report on a subject as controversial as the international response to the Ethiopian drought could merit a foreword. Jack Shepherd's report requires one because it is the product of an Endowment experiment and an example of how one project can fortuitously lead to another.

The experiment began with the Endowment's International Fact Finding Center in New York. Started in late April 1974, the Center provides an opportunity for foreign affairs professionals, usually journalists, to undertake investigative, anticipatory research on pre-crisis issues which carry significant threats to peaceful international relations. Bureaucracies tend to let the pressures of immediate crises draw up the agenda of issues for them. Those of the pre-crisis stage are often overlooked. The hope is that by matching experienced people and appropriate subjects on a limited number of issues, the Center may on occasion be able to fill an information gap—in the modest ways open to a non-governmental organization—between the newspaper headlines on today's crisis and the scholarly studies of that crisis after it has passed into history.

Mr. Shepherd is a professional journalist who has specialized in African politics and environmental questions. A former senior editor of *Look*, he has traveled widely in East Africa. With another colleague, Professor Tom J. Farer, he joined the Endowment to study what we then saw as an emerging political crisis in the Horn of Africa—the opening of the Suez Canal, the enhanced great power interest in the Indian Ocean, and the changing political and military structure within several countries in the Horn. As they conducted their research (which will result in a separate study by Mr. Farer), countless international civil servants persuaded Mr. Shepherd and Mr. Farer that in the international community's response to the Ethiopian drought, there could be found an almost classic case of the past saying something important about the future. As those civil servants pointed out, today the United Nations Disaster Relief Organization in Geneva is announcing international disasters requiring international assistance at the rate of two or three a month. We have, in short, an alarm bell going off regularly with no one listening until the human cost of international disregard becomes so enormous that the international press becomes involved in the matter. At that point, however, it is too late for thousands, perhaps even tens of thousands, who have already starved. Moreover, the efforts undertaken in the glare of international press publicity sometimes seem more designed to end the publicity than to aid the afflicted. So this separate report on the drought developed.

Mr. Shepherd's report is not an indictment of individuals, but a description of how diplomatic routine and high level inhibitions continued to paralyze the international community in Ethiopia long after the human cost of inaction became evident and even unconscionable. Yet, as this report suggests, the same routine and the same inhibitions probably will paralyze the international community again unless serious changes are made.

In fact, at the moment this foreword is being written, history seems to be repeating itself in Ethiopia. The government there is locked into a life and death struggle with the liberation forces in the province of Eritrea. To eliminate the possibility that these forces might indirectly benefit from international relief efforts, in August, 1975, the government ordered them stopped. Once again, therefore, UN agencies face the dilemma of remaining silent to protect existing programs favored by the government or speaking out to draw international attention to the pending crisis with no assurance that anyone will listen.

It is in this light that the institutional recommendations contained in the afterward should be viewed. Its author is Stephen Green, the UNICEF officer in Ethiopia during the period of the drought, who with a few others, when the disparity between the needs of the Ethiopian people and the international response to those needs rose to an intolerable point, broke ranks and called the attention of the world press to the true dimensions of the disaster taking place in Ethiopia. For the past year, Mr. Green has been investigating possible institutional reforms which the international community might undertake to insure that its response will never again be as inadequate and as misguided as it was in Ethiopia during the past few years. Together Mr. Shepherd's report and Mr. Green's afterword amount to description and recommendation mutually supporting one another.

There will be other interpretations of what happened in Ethiopia during the period studied. Different solutions from those proposed in this report will be advanced. As always, Endowment sponsorship of the report implies a belief only in the importance of the subject. The views expressed are necessarily those of the authors.

Comments or inquiries on this and other work of the Endowment are welcome and may be addressed to the offices of the Carnegie Endowment for International Peace, 345 East 46th Street, New York, New York 10017; or 11 Dupont Circle, Washington, D.C. 20036.

Thomas L. Hughes
President
Carnegie Endowment for
International Peace

INTRODUCTION

It took less than twenty-four months to end the 2,000-year-old Ethiopian empire.

During those months, between 1973 and 1975, the rush of events in Ethiopia outpaced detailed study. In 1973, and even before, drought spread to famine beneath an official coverup; civil and military dissatisfactions fed a creeping coup that took a year to topple Haile Selassie at age eighty-two, along with his forty-four-year-old government. A new Military Council executed some of its opponents; stepped up the war against Eritrean guerrillas; asked for (and received) a shipment of military aid from an old ally, the United States; and issued details of a land reform program, then dispatched khaki-uniformed students into the bush to carry it out.

Most of the attention Ethiopia attracted during this period has focused upon the traditional issues: the changing strategic importance of the Horn; the roles of the United States, the Soviet Union, France, and China; and the value of the Horn's bases for major powers sailing the Indian Ocean, Red Sea, or Persian Gulf.

Overlooked by the rapid progression of events and the high-politics thinking was the profound effect of the drought, famine, and coverup that shattered the Ethiopian people and altered their living patterns as surely as any revolution. Drought and famine continue, spreading southward. Recovery in the Horn will come slowly, if at all, and only with the long-term aid of the developed countries. Arguments may be made that the drought and famine triggered the unrest that led to Haile Selassie's downfall, that the Imperial Ethiopian government's (IEG) indifference to and coverup of such widespread suffering served as a focal point for Ethiopian dissidents, that a feudalistic regime proved inadequate to the responsibilities of a modern state. (In fact, one of the first acts of the coup leaders was to investigate and accuse members of the IEG, including the Emperor, for the famine and coverup.*)

A true apportionment of responsibility, however, has to this day been avoided. Neither have the lessons learned in Ethiopia been applied to the realities of international diplomacy. Close investigation of the 1973-74 coup reveals not one but two coverups. The first by the IEG, has been widely, but not fully, reported. The second, by the international relief agencies and donor nations, has not previously been examined.

The second coverup is, of course, equally condemning. It was one thing for the IEG to act slowly: it believed drought and famine "normal" for Ethiopia; it lacked the administrative skills to implement drought aid quickly; it didn't wish to appear like "just another Sahel"; and some of its ministers (and perhaps the Emperor himself) held back public pleas for aid in the hope that the December, 1973, harvest would be good and save them the embarrassment.

But the relief agencies, both national and multinational, have no such excuses. They attract and hire top bureaucrats, who can mobilize worldwide efforts to relieve hunger and disease. From headquarters in Geneva, Rome, New York, and the great capitals of the world, these bureaucrats can alert distracted national governments to issues of global

---

*Prime minister Aklilu Habte Wold resigned on February 27, 1974, in the face of a growing armed forces revolt. He was followed by Endalkachew Makonnen, who was arrested August 1, 1974, and replaced by Michael Imru. On August 27, 1974, a fifteen-man Commission of Inquiry published its charges against the Habte Wold government. The commission unanimously condemned the entire government for its handling of "the problem of drought," and, in a fifteen-page statement, accused the Habte Wold cabinet of deliberately suppressing all news about the famine and drought and of being guilty of neglect. It ordered that the former prime minister and thirty-four people who served under him, including Legesse Bezu, the former minister of the interior and then governor-general of Wollo from late 1973 to mid-1974, stand trial.

In its report, the commission implicated Haile Selassie, who was himself arrested on September 12, 1974. It said that Mamo Seyoum, while governor and special imperial envoy in Wollo, had written to Selassie in August, 1970, warning him of the effects of the drought and asking that he take urgent steps to save the lives of thousands of starving peasants. The commission said that Mamo Seyoum had pressed Prime Minister Aklilu Habte Wold, the Crown Prince, and the Emperor about this matter for four years. Nothing had been done.

concern. They can seek necessary mandates and with them can coordinate and offer doctors, nurses, a whole spectrum of relief workers, and— most importantly— shiploads of relief supplies to drought-stricken areas like Ethiopia.

But these agencies, these men and women, chose not to act. As evidence of drought and famine became widely known in Addis Ababa, these agencies remained silent. Their reason—their only excuse—was diplomatic tradition and practice. For in the international community, no aid is given or even offered, regardless of the consequences, without the specific request and the cooperation of the recipient country. In Ethiopia, as long as the IEG covered up the drought, the international community went along with its own coverup and remained silent despite what its members knew was happening to the Ethiopian people.

It was one thing, therefore, for the IEG to turn its back. But for these agencies to go along with the IEG was something else. They knew about the drought, and they had the international obligation to raise questions privately with the IEG about its seeking drought aid. At some point— when the suffering reached unacceptable levels—they had the obligation to raise these questions publicly. Would this be unwarranted interference in the internal affairs of a state? Were Ethiopian lives expendable to maintain traditional diplomatic practice of noninterference? Debates over these questions went on within several international and national agencies, including UNICEF and the World Health Organization (WHO), among the lower-echelon members, and sometimes between the lower and upper, more conservative, echelons. Would drought relief have poured into Ethiopia—and lives been saved—had these agencies pressured the IEG and spoken out? The answer is an unequivocal, Yes.

The defense of traditional diplomatic practice missed a major point. The argument that speaking out would have interfered with Ethiopia's internal affairs was weak. For in fact, the drought that swept Ethiopia in 1973, and which persists today, knew no national boundaries. Starving nomads wandered into Kenya, the Sudan, Somalia, and the French Territory of the Afars and Issas. The drought and starvation, therefore, were international in character and required both the voice and the power of the international community to deal with them.

Instead, the international community remained silent and created the second coverup. Behind the protective curtain of respect for local sovereignty, the second coverup went along with the IEG's own coverup and involved every major international relief agency, most donor nations, and many African leaders. All kept quiet as the Selassie government requested. One authoritative voice might have saved thousands; their silence condemned tens of thousands.

One international relief official who was in Ethiopia during the crisis—and didn't speak out—ticked off a list of partners in silence: the American embassy, one of the largest in Africa, which included more than twenty-five United States Aid for International Development (USAID) workers in Addis Ababa alone; the West Germans, Swedes, British; the French, a colonial power with important railroad connections in nearby Djibouti, but who never donated a single bag of their wheat surpluses of 1973-74; the leaders of the Organization for African Unity (OAU), who wined and dined in Addis amid the worst of the famine, and who knew about it (but didn't believe the reports); and the UN agencies—the Food and Agriculture Organization (FAO), silent despite its own advance crop warnings; WHO, which also deliberately and carefully covered up a massive cholera outbreak; UNICEF, whose workers in the field cabled, argued, fought, and finally resigned from its reluctant bureaucracy. "The inability of these international organizations and nations to halt the famine, aid the people and do what they are set up to do," said the U.S. official in Addis, "is the most shocking part of it all."

But how to speak out? Addis is a center for journalists in Africa. So is Nairobi, Kenya, an hour's flight away. Information and reports could have been given, "leaked," to them—a system that international agencies practice as an art when they wish. In fact, the coverup of the famine later on was exposed by English journalists, and it may be argued that only then did the international outcry pressure Haile Selassie to visit the drought-stricken areas and open his country to aid.

Beginning in early 1973, what happened, briefly, was this:

From April to November, 1973, Haile Selassie's government persistently denied that any widespread starvation was taking place in Ethiopia. Publicly, there was no famine. The government would not be embarrassed. By May, 1973, when the OAU met in splendor for its tenth anniversary celebration in Addis Ababa, officials in every international agency and embassy in the capital knew what was happening to Ethiopia's people. Some agencies, including the United Nations, had documented it, and U.S. embassy cables to Washington were detailing the famine graphically. So presumably had cables flowing into other major capitals. Yet not one agency or nation—no one—spoke out.

In the Sahel, the bungling of food supplies for starving West Africans had come about largely because of bureaucratic inefficiency. In Ethiopia, the delays in shipping relief food came not from bureaucratic foul-up, but from diplomatic choice. Unlike the Sahel, where widespread breakdowns in famine relief were accidental, in Ethiopia there was a simple, deliberate choice: to convince the Ethiopian government of the seriousness of its problem and start relief aid pouring in, or to go along with the IEG's coverup.

Between April and November, 1973, everyone decided to go quietly along. Not until November, when Haile Selassie went to Wollo Province and proclaimed shock at what he saw, was the famine allowed to become public, and the relief foods started coming in. During those seven months of silence, however, a crisis became a catastrope, and more than 100,000 Ethiopians starved to death.

This was not the first time that starving Ethiopian peasants had been ignored. But this famine, the worst in the Horn since 1916, came at a special time. By 1973, national problems of drought and starvation took on unprecedented international urgency. These catastrophes no longer affected only a single nation, but whole regions and continents. In Africa alone, fifty million people were hurt by the drought, and starvation spread from the Atlantic Ocean to the Red Sea.

In Ethiopia, by 1974, peasants were starving in at least eleven provinces. Another two million Ethiopians, according to an unpublished UN Food and Agriculture Organization report prepared in late 1974, were "completely destitute." When a final tally is made by the end of 1975, perhaps as many as 500,000 people will have starved to death in Africa's Horn, five times the number of Africans who starved in all of West Africa's Sahel.

The drought and subsequent famine caused serious long-term damage to Ethiopia. Traditional patterns of society have been broken; in some areas there was little for the Ethiopian peasant to return to: whole villages dead; *awrajas,* or districts, deserted; a way of life shattered. Even today, vast populations of abandoned mothers with children roam the land. Can Ethiopia be helped beyond simple emergency aid? Erosion and overgrazing have decimated her agricultural soil; some land may never be arable again. A 1974 Ethiopian government report concludes: "The ecological balance has been seriously disturbed," the land's ability to sustain life "has been severely curtailed." The unpublished United Nations FAO report, reveals that, through 1985, food shortages, malnutrition, and disease will stalk the Ethiopian people. But what does this mean for the future of Ethiopia and the Horn? How much outside aid will be needed, who will supply it, and for how long?

Ethiopia's catastrophe may be a microcosm of catastrophes now threatening whole regions, such as the Indian subcontinent. An examination of events in Ethiopia shows to what extent international agencies and nations are able or even willing to handle crises that are becoming increasingly commonplace.

Clearly, the drought has become a regional crisis of people. By mid-

1975, the Ethiopian Military Council had placed the number of starving people in the south alone at 200,000.* To the west, in the Sudan, 50,000 nomads in Bahr el Gazal had been hurt by the drought. A new wave of human suffering had swept Kenya and Tanzania to the south. In 1975, 230,000 Somalis were relocated in relief camps, and the Somali ambassador to the European Economic Community (EEC) pled for $9 million in famine relief for his nation. Kurt Waldheim's warning in 1974 that the region "might become the widest mass starvation in recorded history" was moving rapidly toward reality.

---

*By "starving" I mean people near death from lack of food. By "hungry" I mean people with only enough food to keep them barely alive; these would also be malnourished. In Ethiopia alone, at least 100,000 people starved to death in 1973 alone; by 1975, perhaps another 100,000 had starved, and 200,000 were in some stage of starvation—without food—while almost two million were perpetually hungry.

Senator Edward Kennedy to the Reverend George R. Matzat, Lutheran World Relief during the 1974 U.S. Senate Hearings on World Hunger.

"I suppose . . . the problem, in looking back, is why the whistle was not really sounded on this [famine coverup] before. It appears to me that the voluntary agencies were aware of it. The U.S. Government should have known about it.

But because it was not sounded, there are going to be a lot of people . . . that are going to pay for it with their lives."

Reverend Matzat: "That is correct."

I

In the middle of February, 1973, a raggedy band of 1,500 Ethiopian peasants appeared on the outskirts of Addis Ababa. Police halted them there and demanded an explanation. The peasant-farmers told a shocking story. They described the poor harvests around their villages in Wollo Province, some 200 miles north of Addis Ababa. They detailed the repeated failure of the seasonal rains; how they couldn't plant seeds for the harvests; how their plow oxen had weakened and starved; and how, in desperation, they had had to eat their seed grain instead of planting it. Those who owned land sold it for a few dollars. Others sold their animals, their tools, the wood from their huts, even their clothes. But when the hunger continued, sweeping over whole villages and districts, the men reluctantly left their women and children and began a frightening search for food.

Word of their arrival filtered up to the minister of the interior, who asked the governor-general of Wollo to explain the presence of these shabbily-dressed peasants outside Ethiopia's capital city. The governor-general, Solomon Abraham, an old aristocrat and political appointee, assured the Imperial government that, while there was some "problem of drought" in Wollo, there was little cause for concern. And when the Imperial government sent an official inspection team to Wollo and Tigre provinces to investigate, the team returned to reassure everyone that only 1,500 peasants were "affected by a shortage of food." The word famine wasn't even mentioned.

After all, the IEG reasoned, hadn't Ethiopian peasants always starved before the harvests? In 1958-59, perhaps 100,000 of them had quietly starved to death in the northern and central provinces, and few Imperial government officials or international relief workers had cared then. According to tradition, the Ethiopian people obeyed their Emperor, their Imperial government, their Orthodox Church—they starved quietly.

In 1973, however, this tradition also died. For these marching Ethiopian peasants were a signal: 2,000 years of empire were ending; a feudal society was crumbling.

For centuries, the people of Wollo and neighboring Tigre Province had shaped the history of their homeland. Wollo and Tigre had formed the heart of ancient Ethiopia. The great kings and emperors have ruled from these provinces since the tenth century B.C. From Axum, in Tigre, the Queen of Sheba is said to have begun her journey to Jerusalem and King Solomon; and their son, Menelik I, is believed to be the first in a line of rulers that included Haile Selassie, the 226th descendant. Here, too, first appeared the Ethiopian Orthodox Church, even today the most dominant and powerful Christian church in the nation. Along the Lasta Mountains in Wollo, gifted craftsmen of the medieval King Lalibela carved into the rock—some say with the help of angels—a dozen churches still used today. But these magnificent mountain enclaves also isolated the Ethiopians, and they became, in Gibbon's famous phrase, "Forgetful of the world, by whom they were forgotten."

This land, harsh and dominant, also shaped the history of the "Forgotten Empire." Parts of Wollo rise to 15,000 feet and form the backbone of Ethiopia, running north-south down the center of the province. In the highlands, fertile plateaus cut by eroded canyons thousands of feet deep fall away to populated foothills, which in turn slope toward sparsely populated savannah. Beyond the savannah stretches the great Danakil Desert, undulating eastward to the Red Sea. The mountains, deep canyons and plateaus, savannah, and desert separate the people and their villages. The peasants travel by foot or mule along footpaths to reach their only link to a distant world, the vital two-lane Addis Ababa-Asmara highway—one of the few tarmac roads in all of Ethiopia.

Strung along the Addis-Asmara highway, which bisects Wollo and Tigre, are villages and market towns with romantic names like Debre Birhan, Kobbo, Alamata, Adigat. This artery sustains life in the distant *awrajas* and villages. Here, peasants trade news from the interior. Christian farmers from the highlands and nomadic Moslem herdsmen from the desert barter and sell sheep, goats, cattle, cloth, sorghum, corn, wheat—the things of life. Here, too, in the coming drought, they would find death: these market villages would mark their burial grounds like tombstones.

Birth and death, the seasons, the timeless cycle of crops measure the lives of these people. Rain patterns dictate that Tigre has just one planting season, May to August. But in most parts of Wollo, there are two seasons: the short, or *belq*, crop of wheat, barley, and pulses, planted in February and harvested in June; and the long season, from June or July to December, when teff, wheat, barley, and other crops are planted and harvested.

For the people of Tigre and Wollo, who numbered about 4.2 million before the drought, little changes.* The death of emperors, the court and government intrigues of distant Addis Ababa seldom touch them. Almost all of them, like peasants everywhere in Ethiopia, live at the hard edge of existence.

In Wollo, before the drought, there were 375,000 landless peasants, and more than 90,000 of them paid at least half and perhaps three-quarters of their produce as tribute to their landlords. In addition, the landlord often got one-tenth of the gross produce. Equally bad, the Ministry of Finance still gets most of its taxation revenue from farmers earning less than $300 a year.

Who were the landlords? Before any land reform was carried out, the State, the Crown, and the Ethiopian Orthodox Church were the largest. One survey showed that a single Ethiopian landlord held more than two million acres of fertile land and received up to three-quarters of the produce grown on it. In 1973, some 27 per cent of all landlords were absentees; most of these were either Ethiopian nobility or officials rewarded for favors to the Emperor. Before the famine and the military coup, only 5 per cent of the total registered land in Tigre and Wollo had been distributed to the peasant-farmers; 95 per cent had been given to officials and other elite, largely, according to a study by the Royal Africa Society in 1973, "to reduce opposition and secure loyalty to the political system."

That system exacerbated the nation's other disparities. While their Emperor invited the OAU and the Economic Commission for Africa to build modern headquarters in Addis, the Ethiopian peasants lived in mud huts. Nine out of ten of the people outside the capital subsisted on farming, deeply entrenched in an ancient semifeudal system and earning about $82 a year—in a good year. They were ruled by an aging emperor,

---

*Because there has been no accurate census in Ethiopia, and birth statistics are not kept, all population in figures should be carefully regarded. I have tried to be as conservative in selecting and using figures as possible.

but their average age was just fifteen. And while Haile Selassie was glorified as a world leader, his subjects cultivated the soil with wooden plows. The Emperor toured world capitals, but eight out of ten of his people lived a full day's walk from any road.

Of the twenty-five nations designated by the United Nations as least developed, Ethiopia has the third largest population (twenty-six million), the lowest literacy rate (about 5 per cent, but only 0.6 per cent for women), and the fewest doctors—just one for every 250,000 people. One U.S. embassy official adds with dismay: "The health sector is a disaster. It's oriented to keeping the nobility healthy in the urban areas."

How could this be? More than any other African nation, Ethiopia has been closely linked with the outside world, through its role in the United Nations and the OAU, its relationship with France at Djibouti, and through its close and friendly ties with the United States. In the case of the United States, diplomatic relations began in 1903. U.S. and world admiration for Haile Selassie deepened when, on June 30, 1936, while his country was under attack by Italian forces, he implored the League of Nations to honor "the value of promises made to small states that their integrity and their independence shall be respected and assured."

Western admiration wasn't lessened in 1950 when the Emperor sent three thousand Ethiopian combat troops to fight in Korea or, during the late 1950's and 1960's, when Haile Selassie used his influence with the OAU to support projects that most of the leading powers in the world also felt were important. He was a mediator most diplomats, in Africa and outside, could trust. He averted an international crisis in 1963 by mediating the border dispute between Algeria and Morocco. He worked quietly to avoid a grave split among African nations and bring peace to a Nigeria torn by civil war. During the several years of the Congo crisis, Haile Selassie twice sent his troops and jets in action supporting UN objectives. As for U.S. attitudes toward Ethiopia, as David Newsom, then assistant secretary of state for African affairs told a congressional subcommittee in 1971: "We have always considered. . . that the general importance to us of the Emperor, of the key position of Ethiopia, [of] the need to keep it friendly in the total African context were justification for our programs in Ethiopia."

What programs? Soon after the Emperor sent Ethiopian troops to Korea, the United States entered into two major agreements, signed May 22, 1953. One agreement permitted the United States to build and operate until 1978 an intelligence and defense communications base at Kagnew outside Asmara, the provincial capital of Eritrea. Kagnew, now slowly being replaced by satellites, became a major relay station for worldwide U.S. defense communications. At its peak use, in 1972-73, the Department of Defense kept 1,805 employees at Kagnew busy watching the Middle East, the Indian Ocean, the Persian Gulf, Africa, and other regions.

In exchange, the second agreement (inextricably weaving the United States into the fabric of Ethiopian politics) outlined a major military program for the Ethiopian armed forces. Soon these close relations with Haile Selassie were involving the United States, and thus its competitors, in a distant and complicated corner of the world.

As rent for Kagnew, the United States developed a major aid program for the Ethiopians. Since 1953, the United States has provided more than $230 million in economic aid. In twenty-two years, the United States has passed on to Ethiopia some $170 million in military aid—by far the largest amount of U.S. arms in all of Africa. This does not include sales of arms for cash, which constitute the bulk of international arms agreements. America has trained 2,813 Ethiopians, mostly officers and pilots, in the United States at an additional cost of $6.8 million.

A U.S. Military Assistance Advisory Group (MAAG) office was opened in Addis Ababa in 1953. Between 1953 and 1960, the United States through MAAG trained and armed three Ethiopian divisions of six thousand men each. In 1960, however, the Emperor made a case for a sharp increase in his military strength. That year, the Somali Republic was formed out of former British and Italian Somalilands, and its leaders called for the unity of all Somalis, including a large number who happened to graze their livestock in Ethiopia's Ogaden Desert. Also in 1960, dissident Ethiopians attempted a coup. Haile Selassie voiced concern over the "Somali threat" to the south and insurrection inside his kingdom, and the United States armed and trained a fourth Ethiopian division, and the size of all four divisions was increased so that the number of Ethiopians under arms rose to forty thousand.

Thereafter, Ethiopia and the United States made military agreements in 1960, 1962, 1963, 1964, and on, every year through 1975. U.S. military equipment poured in: armored personnel carriers; trucks; M-1 rifles; jeeps mounted with recoilless rifles; .50- and .30-cal. machine guns; F-86 jet fighters; C-47s and L-19s; T-28 and T-33 jet trainers; UH-1H helicopters; C-54s; and, in 1964, twelve F-5As, the first supersonic jet fighters in black or East Africa.

Along with American equipment came American soldiers. The MAAG outfit grew to a brigadier general, five full colonels, seventeen lieutenant colonels, twenty-one majors, three captains, a warrant officer, and fifty-three enlisted men by 1971—the largest U.S. military group on the African continent.* The MAAG ran tight offices in Addis Ababa; in Harar, near the Somali border; and at Asmara and Massawa, in the rebellious Eritrea Province. All of this, according to the U.S. military assistance presentation book, was necessary to help Haile Selassie "maintain internal security."

During the 1960's, Ethiopian insurgents tangled with the Emperor's troops in Bale, Sidamo, Tigre, and Eritrea. In Eritrea, stubborn guerrilla fighting broke out.

In 1964, as the Eritrean Liberation Front (ELF) grew bolder, another kind of American military adviser showed up in Ethiopia: 55 U.S. soldiers in a counterinsurgency team began training selected Ethiopian troops to combat the guerrillas. In 1966, Plan Delta brought 164 U.S. soldiers for two- or three-year hitches to teach counterinsurgency to the Ethiopians. A twelve-man "counterinsurgency civic action advisory team" was sent in to organize units of the Ethiopian army into antiguerrilla teams. None of the Americans wore Green Berets, but it was obvious who they were and what they were doing.

As in Vietnam, antiguerrilla tactics had little success and alarming consequences. U.S.-trained Ethiopian counter-insurgency teams attacked villages in Eritrea and arrested suspected ELF members. In December, 1970, the peasants of a small village outside Keren were accused of sheltering ELF forces. All the peasants—600 Ethiopians—were systematically killed by the Emperor's antiguerrilla army teams. Other villages were burned down and the inhabitants marched off to refugee camps.

By 1971, perhaps prophetically in light of the larger human tragedy which would soon unfold, Senator Stuart Symington had examined these details and concluded: ". . . We are sitting in the middle of a mess." But it got worse. By the time of the drought, the United States was deeply committed to Haile Selassie and his "Forgotten Empire." Its officials recalled ". . . the value of promises made to small states" and the pledge, made in the 1960 arms agreement with Ethiopia, that "the United States Government also reaffirmed its continued interest in the security of Ethiopia and its opposition to any activities threatening the territorial integrity of Ethiopia."

Not that the U.S. government was alone in the importance it attached to the Emperor's remaining in power. The IEG enjoyed unique stature in many world capitals. In addition to aid from the United States, Haile Selassie collected $16.24 million from Italy for World War II

---

*In 1975, MAAG still has fifty officers and enlisted men stationed in Ethiopia and is still the largest in Africa. The U.S. embassy, the Peace Corps, USAID, and other official agencies are among the largest found in any nation of Africa.

reparations and, between 1960 and 1970, another $36.8 million from other donors. Not enough of it went into economic development. Few journalists measured the impact of this aid on the Ethiopian people. And none, until the Eritrean blowup of 1975, questioned the use of U.S. arms against rebellious Ethiopians or the depth to which a superpower had committed itself to maintain Ethiopia's security and internal affairs.

The World Bank maintains that to develop at all a country must have a growth rate of at least 6 per cent per year. But while economic aid flowed into Ethiopia, her growth rate stagnated at just 2 per cent per year. Between 1962 and 1971, Ethiopian agriculture, upon which nine out of ten of her people depend for their livelihood, grew just 2.2 per cent, or about the same rate as the total population. In some rural areas the growth rate was negative. Still, the U.S. government touted Ethiopia as the potential "breadbasket for the Middle East."

In all, the United States gave Haile Selassie more than $400 million in economic and military assistance, all but $40 million of that since 1961. But few Americans were asking whether aid from the United States and other nations was effectively changing life in Ethiopia. Instead, the American and European press tended to praise the little Emperor and Ethiopia's advances into "the modern era." According to one U.S. publication in 1967, Haile Selassie had propelled his people "into the modern world for the first time after centuries of darkness."*

News of this emergence never reached the peasants. By early 1973, the breadbasket had become the beggar's bowl.

---

*Ray Vicker, *The Wall Street Journal*, February 10, 1967.

II

Wollo was the disfavored province. Aristocrats in Wollo had long thought that they had a better claim to the throne than Haile Selassie. The Emperor regarded them as upstarts and threats and the people as potentially disloyal. This animosity between ruler and subject—between Amhara and Galla—had a particularly bitter manifestation. On May 2, 1936, during the Italian War, as Haile Selassie retreated from Addis Ababa, the peasants of Wollo and the Danakil attacked and spat upon him. The Emperor was not one to forget such things.

So Wollo became the forgotten province of the "Forgotten Empire." Haile Selassie sent its people the Crown Prince, Asfa Wossen, and that was supposed to be good enough for them. Asfa Wossen owned an entire valley in Wollo and 28,000 acres of fertile bottom land. The produce of this land was shipped to Addis Ababa. Wollo had few schools and a single hospital with only 125 beds. There were no secondary roads, and its interior villages remained distant and inaccessible.

Few roads had been built anywhere in Ethiopia since the Italian occupation, with the exception of recent U.S., Swedish, and British Food-for-Work projects in Tigre and Eritrea. There was never a national road-building program nor any agency to plan or implement such a scheme. The lack of roads would be a serious obstacle to getting relief food to starving people

Only in Tigre had a secondary road network been built. Ras Mengasha Seyoum, the governor-general, personally drove bulldozers and supervised the construction of 2,700 kilometers of feeder roads which would, in 1973-74, help get food to his people and hold down the number of peasants who starved to death to half that in neighboring Wollo. Ras Mengasha was married to Haile Selassie's granddaughter and therefore an Ethiopian with the imprimatur of authority and tradition. He was, said a diplomat grudgingly, "a politician of the people, which is almost unheard of in Ethiopia where politicians build networks of fear."

No politician stopped what was happening to the land, however, and the coming tragedy was clearly of man's making. For almost two decades, the people along the highlands of Wollo and Tigre had been pushing out to more and more marginal land. As the people increased, so did their animals. Ethiopia before the drought had the largest animal population of any African nation—between sixty-five and seventy-five million head of livestock. Most were cattle, goats, and sheep; while sheep and goats account for much of the meat supply in rural areas, they are also notorious overgrazers. Large portions of Ethiopia are overgrazed and, as the drought began and the pasture diminished, what remained was badly abused.

Centuries of careless land use had already stripped Ethiopia's topsoil. Fifty years ago, perhaps 60 per cent of Ethiopia was covered with forests. The trees held the soil and protected the watershed. Gradually, Ethiopia's forests were cut, mainly for firewood. Increased deforestation led to severe water run-off, floods, and erosion. Today, only 5 per cent of Ethiopia is forest land. The topsoil, so vital to an agricultural nation, is quickly washing into the sea. As one diplomat in Addis put it: "Ethiopia is vanishing; its soil is floating away. As the soil goes down, the population goes up, and that means catastrophe."

The primary causes of the drought and the famine, therefore, were not simply climatic, but also developmental and political. The preconditions of the famine were rooted in Ethiopia's archaic structure and land tenure system. A USAID report in 1974 stated: "The [land] tenure system helps assure that the peasantry will follow and perpetuate—because he has no incentive not to—those defective agricultural practices—lack of soil and water conservation, lack of afforestation and reforestation, lack of crop rotation, lack of fodder crops and stock control, etc.—which encourage and abet the ecological deficiencies which eventuate the drought."

But who could expect peasants, always near starvation, to worry about ecology? As long as the onerous sharecropper or tenant system existed throughout the agricultural sections of the empire, soil erosion and overgrazing would be accepted as facts of a life spent scrambling for food. The oppression, the subsistence, the farm credit system, the court system favoring the landowner over the peasant, the tax system—all forced the peasant to harvest his crops and market them immediately, and eat whatever he could find until the next harvest. This vast system held—and still will hold until land reform becomes effective—the majority of Ethiopians on the bitter edge of life. No rain, or poor crops, plunge them into catastrophe.

One alarming aspect of the drought, therefore, was that its underlying causes went far beyond the mere failure of rains and crops. In a pessimistic, but candid, report circulated privately in late November, 1973, as the drought and famine were slowly being made public, the Ethiopian government admitted: "Throughout Tigre and good parts of Wollo and elsewhere, the ecological balance has been seriously disturbed. . . . Long settlement has meant progressive deforestation and soil erosion. While the capacity of the soil to produce and to sustain human and livestock existence has been severely curtailed, the human and livestock population has grown, and grown rapidly, in recent years. One of the results of this imbalance has been the present famine."

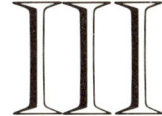

The peasants and farmers knew bad times were coming. For a decade, the rains had failed or had come in torrents, flooding the fields. Planting had been very difficult. In 1970, only light rains fell. The harvest at the end of 1971 was poor, and a small amount of surplus grain was sent by the Imperial government to Gemu Gofa, Wollo, Kaffa, Gojjam, and Tigre provinces. The peasants began eating whatever food reserves they had. In 1972, the harvests again were poor. In Tigre alone, five of eight *awrajas* had harvests that a UN report said ranged from "below average" to "total loss." In five provinces, many farmers were without seed in 1972. The IEG's Ministry of Agriculture estimated that 7,500 tons of seed were needed to allow full planting for 1973, but the Imperial government distributed only 500 tons.

In 1973, many peasants harvested nothing and did not even get their seed back. At the same time, the drought blistered grazing lands and weakened plow oxen. Thus, by the time of the long rains in 1973—which, ironically, caused severe erosion and damaged crops—there were few strong oxen for planting and little seed. Failure of the crops deepened and intensified the starvation, and famine and disease fell upon two million people in Ethiopia's most agriculturally productive provinces. Tigre and Wollo, before the drought, had supplied as much as 40 per cent of the country's total food crops.

On November 15, 1972, the Planning and Programming Department of the Ethiopian Ministry of Agriculture sent to the minister, Kassa

Wolde-Mariam, its annual crop survey. The cold statistics detailed serious crop failures in Wollo and Tigre provinces. And the report clearly warned: "It is most likely that the seriously reduced yields expected in these areas will bring about widespread food shortages."

The report named specific *awrajas* of Wollo and Tigre, predicted that they would suffer food shortages in 1973, and described how these shortages would occur and how widespread they would be. It was a sharp, advance warning, and it came from an excellent source: the Ministry of Agriculture's crop reporting system was the best there was in a country where little statistical reporting is done at all.

Kassa' Wolde-Mariam dutifully passed along the report to Ethiopia's cabinet, the Council of Ministers. There, however, it met an icy reception. The minister of agriculture was told in early 1973 that under no circumstances should the annual crop survey be made public. He was neither to circulate nor publish the document, and he agreed. The IEG's coverup was beginning.

By April, 1973, when the peasant-farmers marched to the edge of Addis with their warning, the Imperial Ethiopian government already knew that drought and famine were spreading—not only in Tigre and Wollo provinces, but also in Begemdir, Harrarghe, and parts of Shoa, where Addis Ababa itself is located. Reports from provincial officials began reaching the government. In Addis, the UN Food and Agriculture Organization prepared, with the assistance of the Ministry of Agriculture, an estimate that 60,000 metric tons of grain would be needed in the second half of 1973 to make good previous harvest failures. More junior members of the Imperial government quickly grasped the rapidly approaching crisis. With a desperation unmatched before—or since—they quietly circulated a letter through the major international relief agencies in Addis Ababa. It contained a prophetic plea:

"The famine situation is rapidly getting worse and more people are exected to face the problems of food and water shortage. Indeed, the scale of the problem has reached such a proportion that prompt and adequate assistance has to be obtained . . . we hope that our request will gain your favourable support and prompt consideration on account of the extreme urgency of the matter and the acuteness of the famine situation."

The letter, coming from proud and sensitive—albeit junior—officials of the IEG, should have rung alarm bells in every relief agency and embassy in Addis. But in large part because those issuing the warning were junior, nothing was done. Indeed, only one major agency sought to investigate the extent of the famine, and some small supplies already in Ethiopia were diverted by the IEG to the northern provinces. On April

13, 1973, the IEG imposed a ban on the export of cereal grains except, under license, to limited traditional markets, mainly the adjoining Territory of the Afars and Issas (Djibouti), which was also feeling the drought. Then the IEG, having issued its warning at a junior level, relaxed. The suspicion in diplomatic circles two years later was that older ministers, and perhaps the Emperor himself, had underestimated (or overlooked) the impact of the drought and hoped that a good harvest and traditionally docile peasants would see them over the situation. The IEG announced that "an on-the-spot investigation" had led to a "distribution for free this week in the drought-stricken area" of food, milk, and medical supplies. Everything was under control.

So began a strange and deadly game. In April, 1973, the IEG reactivated the old National Emergency Relief Committee (NERC), a dormant body of cabinet ministers and government officials formed originally in 1971 to give the appearance of dealing with starvation and a cholera outbreak. Ato Mulatu Debebe, minister of community development and social affairs, was appointed its official head. NERC was supposed to mobilize funds and gather supplies.

At first, NERC and other IEG officials did privately contact some international agencies and embassies in Addis Ababa. But these potential donors wanted a public, large-scale meeting of all foreign agencies with the IEG to coordinate and plan a massive relief effort. Such a meeting, in the words of one relief director, "would have let the cat out of the bag." NERC replied with a curt memorandum: "We do not see the need for such a meeting." Ato Mulatu Debebe would spend most of 1973 attacking the press reports detailing the growing horror; and the IEG, as late as February, 1974, would label any assessment of the starvation that emphasized the scale of suffering as "wishful malice."*

To all inquiries about the drought, the IEG replied with strong public denials and stuffiness. To local protests it replied with gunfire.

---

*The National Emergency Relief Committee, late in 1973, published a letter stating that it had collected $1.5 million in cash and kind for relief and food supplies. But it did not say that the majority of that was in kind—trucks, equipment, cost of salaries, and labor. The report listed Haile Selassie as having contributed $117,000; but there was no lump sum shown from the Ethiopian treasury, which had the money. Nor did the report show what happened to $40,000 collected by students at Haile Selassie University in Addis, who had voluntarily given up their breakfasts to raise money. Ethiopia's civil servants were forced by the IEG to contribute 10 per cent of their salaries, a sizeable sum which, according to one account, "disappeared." In 1974, one U.S. embassy official thought the monies were still in NERC's account in the Commercial Bank of Ethiopia in Addis. Wherever the money ended up, USAID, in its unclassified report on the drought, states that it was collected "without visible impact on the drought area."

When Haile Selassie University students attempted to gather at the Addis Ababa campus to discuss the seriousness of the drought and the IEG's inaction, they were violently dispersed by the police. In Dessie, the capital of Wollo Province, police clubbed demonstrators and fired into the crowd. Eight students died from gunshot wounds.* Three professors at Haile Selassie University during the spring of 1973 investigated the impact of the drought and complained about the IEG's indifference at an open alumni association meeting in Addis. They were arrested,** but not before one of them, Mesfin Wolde-Mariam, associate professor of geography, detailed the Imperial Ethiopian government's inaction and charged that its cabinet ministers were willing members of "a private company with unlimited benefits and no accountability."

By June, 1973, the IEG was publicly suppressing discussion of the drought and famine, but at the same time it was privately meeting with potential relief donors. It now wanted large-scale help, but it still wanted it quietly. The IEG and Haile Selassie would not be embarrassed by the publicity attendant with massive inputs of relief foods and supplies. As one State Department official who served in Ethiopia during this period of the famine observed: "The IEG wanted to create the impression that they weren't just another Sahel country coming apart at the seams . . . .".

Among the agencies contacted were the World Food Programme (WFP), UNICEF, FAO, the UN Development Programme (UNDP), and USAID. The game was tricky: the IEG insisted that all of these agencies keep the famine a secret. Should they agree? To respond quickly with offers of massive amounts of grain would raise obvious—and embarrassing—questions and would let the secret out. But keeping quiet and thus preventing a full-scale emergency relief effort from coming in

---

*The shootings at Dessie apparently took place with the approval of the governor-general of Wollo, Solomon Abraham. The incident embarrassed officials in Addis. Solomon Abraham was sacked in June, 1973, and when the IEG needed to explain why it had delayed while people starved, he became a convenient scapegoat. He claimed he had sent reports to the central government about the famine. The IEG accused him of staying in Dessie instead of going out into the province to check on the drought. Wollo officials testified at an IEG inquiry that, during his three-year administration, Solomon Abraham never left Dessie for the rural areas.

**Mesfin Wolde-Mariam was jailed and transferred to a remote job as district governor of the Galla area of Wollo, only to return under the new Military Council to head its Committee of Inquiry into the drought. Dr. Seyoum Gebre Egziabher, professor of political science, was sent off to be mayor of Gondar. Dr. Solomon Unquay, dean of the Extension School, was banished to the USSR as educational attache.

quickly would mean continued and widespread starvation. The choice ultimately involved no choice. For the international agencies and foreign embassies to blow the whistle on the IEG coverup would mean embarrassing an old friend, a respected international figure. It would also mean risking tidy working arrangements between international officials and IEG bureaucrats and threatening delicate projects that had taken years to work out between agency and IEG staffs. Silence was easier than an alarm. The second coverup began.

In April, 1973, IEG officials asked WFP for 20,000 metric tons of grain and USAID for 8,000 metric tons despite its own Ministry of Agriculture (and FAO) estimate that 60,000 metric tons were needed immediately to feed 200,000 hungry Ethiopians.

Both USAID and WFP tried to respond quietly. In May, USAID approved diversion of 2,000 metric tons of Title II Food-for-Work wheat already in the two stricken provinces. Such a move would attract no attention. USAID also agreed to ship 8,000 metric tons of grain for relief aid later. The WFP pledged 20,000 metric tons and asked the United States to fill 10,000 of that; the remainder would be purchased from Kenya or donated by the European Economic Community. Other international donors, among them China and the European countries, also received appeals in April and May, 1973. The total amount of grain pledged was 35,000 metric tons—half the amount needed immediately.

The IEG had quietly appealed. The international donors had quietly pledged. In both cases, the amounts asked and the amounts offered were only fractions of the amounts everyone knew were needed. And that's where the international public relief program ended for most of 1973. By late November, none of the 35,000 metric tons pledged seven months before—by the United States, China, Europe, and WFP—had come in. USAID's pledge, made in May, didn't arrive until December; the 10,000 metric tons donated by the U.S. government (through WFP) began trickling in toward the end of the year and carried into January, 1974. The tardiness was easy to explain. According to Marshall Wright, assistant secretary for congressional relations at the State Department, the U.S. pledge was seven to eight months late ". . . due, in part, to heavy demands on shipping," which U.S. wheat sales to the Soviet Union helped to create.

But in June, 1973, as the growing famine was being detailed at the working level in the American embassy, two U.S. ships carrying Title II wheat for famine relief in Yemen passed near the Ethiopian ports. The IEG quietly asked that one of the ships be diverted to help with the starvation. In response, U.S. officials in Addis Ababa, in a letter to the IEG, said the Ethiopian government would have to "show justification" before any ships would be diverted or extra food brought in. The ships continued to Yemen.

"There was no attempt to inform us or the Ethiopian public of the state of the problem," an unnamed diplomat lamely complained to the *New York Times* almost twelve months later. "Instead, there was a tendency to minimize the problem, as though it was embarrassing." By June, 1973, a horrible famine had been documented. It was well known in almost every international agency and embassy in Addis Ababa, but it was being minimized not only by the IEG but also by officials in those agencies and embassies. While their working-level colleagues went into the field and continued piling up evidence of the mounting disaster, senior officials for governments and international agencies either ignored or misunderstood the human catastrophe around them. They continued to devote their primary attention to political relations with the Ethiopian government. The second coverup continued.

IV

Sometime early in 1973 (no one will ever know exactly when), a mass migration of peasants began deep in the interior of Wollo and Tigre. Almost 90 per cent of their cattle had died. A few had been sold for grain, but grain prices were rising daily and cattle prices dropping, creating, what one UNDP report called "an alarming downward spiral towards destitution." Men went out to search for food. Often they never returned. Some died; some deserted; some reached help but, too ill and malnourished themselves, couldn't get back. Women, children, and the elderly left behind starved in uncounted numbers. The same UNDP report grimly stated: "There are cases where whole communities simply died."

In the spring, tens of thousands of people—first the men, then the women and children, then a few elderly—began straggling into the market towns along the Addis-Asmara highway. By May, 1973, travelers saw them resting beneath stick lean-tos along the roadside. Some died on the highway. Others flagged the vehicles to beg for food. Truckers started complaining that they couldn't get through, and some hauled bags of bread and tossed them out as they sped by.

Young officers of the U.S. embassy in Addis began filing field reports on the latest phase of the deteriorating situation. In time, cables went out to the State Department in Washington, D.C. One, in July, 1973, described the crisis. "Several thousands gather daily at the Dessie provincial headquarters looking for food . . . Some of the migrants traveled up to 200 kilometers in search of relief food. Along the main road," the cable said, "people were . . . forming human chains to stop cars and trucks for food."

A "feeding station" concept was developed by missionaries in Wollo. Churches and missions had been engaged in medical, educational, and social work in northern Ethiopia for decades. When the severity of the drought became known as the peasants gathered at the towns along the Addis-Asmara highway, the missionaries and volunteer relief agencies in Wollo and Tigre started collecting whatever grain they had or could buy and distributing it to peasants at various points along the road.

The IEG and the international community were otherwise occupied. On May 25, 1973, the OAU began celebrating its tenth anniversary in Addis Ababa's Africa Hall, where the OAU was founded in 1963. Some twenty-three heads of state were arriving in the capital. This was no time to mar the celebration. The IEG, aware of the threat to its international reputation, ordered the relief camp at Dessie closed. Thousands of hungry peasants were each handed a small bag of grain and sent back into the interior. There is no public evidence that any of the embassies in Addis Ababa attempted to inform gathering African leaders of the plight of the Ethiopians so that offers of help could be made.

In southern Wollo, peasants seeking food were physically prevented from entering market towns by the local police. While this was happening, Haile Selassie and his visitors enjoyed champagne receptions and lavish banquets. Others turned their backs as well. One nobleman's daughter's ostentatious wedding, held at the same time, featured an extravagant feast at the center of which was a tall and elaborately decorated wedding cake, flown in from England for the occasion. The cake alone cost $3,125; but then it had broken during transit and had had to be repaired, adding to the expense.

In the provinces, the drought and growing famine began to overwhelm the missionaries. The timid international relief agencies and donor nations would argue a year later that the important thing wasn't publicizing the drought and famine, but feeding the people. And who did that? There was little help coming from those agencies or nations. As long as the IEG remained silent, so did they. The peasants were starving quietly, as their patience permitted and as the requirements of international relationships ordained. If the IEG did not admit that it had an emergency, if the international community remained silent, then the bulk of the famine relief work would fall on the voluntary agencies and missionaries.

And so it happened.

As the peasants continued shuffling into the market towns, the church and mission agencies stepped up their feeding programs. On May 19, 1973, twenty religious leaders—no one, however, joining them from the powerful Ethiopian Orthodox Church—met in Addis Ababa to discuss their particular contribution. They agreed to mount their own program "coordinated with the government programme and supplemental to it." These Protestant and Catholic Churchmen—Ethiopians and foreigners—set up the Christian Relief Fund (CRF) with an Irish priest, Father Kevin Doheny, as chairman. This small group, working with various missionaries and volunteers, provided the first substantial aid to the famine victims. In the next seven months, these dedicated churchmen would give more medical and food aid to starving and sick Ethiopians than all the international agencies and donor nations combined.

The Christian Relief Fund made contact with funding sources overseas and started sending whatever aid it could to the provinces. The relief workers plunged in. CRF kept detailed minutes of its weekly meetings in Addis, in effect compiling a history of the famine. Reading these, especially the weekly "Report from the Field," conveys the grim sense of spreading disaster. The first group of relief workers, for example, arriving at the market town of Kobbo, found thousands starving. There were no cooking utensils to feed the large numbers of people, so the workers cut water barrels in two, and "the hungry held pieces of torn plastic sheeting in their hands to receive the hot food."

June 20th, 1973—*Report from the Field.*

"Merca: 30 kms. south of Weldiya. The situation is very serious. People were seen dying of starvation."

"Sheket: It is very difficult to purchase foodstuffs in Asmara for Sheket." 200 quintals purchased by the Seventh Day Adventists at $21 per quintal, but the price is gradually rising up to $26 per quintal in a short time . . .

Massawa area: A Red Sea missionary reports that "the situation south of Massawa has been overlooked and omitted from all records, in spite of very serious famine in that area." Reports from the Danakil indicate that "the condition of the people is really desperate. Cattle, sheep, and goats have almost all died, and the people have practically no food, except what wild fruits they can collect."

June 25th, 1973—*Report from the Field.*

Some 20,000 quintals of grain is supposed to be available for famine relief. But the IEG wants this grain declared unfit for human consumption. It would be sold for feeding livestock . . . Seed being eaten, but "treated with DDT and other evil-smelling compounds to prevent consumption."

Makale: Rev. Kevin Doheny reports that 800 famine victims are in camp at Makale and more arriving every day. Get two meals of Injera and Wat* per day. Gross overcrowding . . . "Many T.B. cases—Skin [sores] resultant from lack of water. All are malnourished. Last week 5 children died . . . The overall picture is very gloomy."

Fr. Kevin O'Mahoney quips: "Our immediate worry is not faith and revelation, but Faffa and water."

By July, sharply rising grain prices were causing a serious problem for CRF, which was buying much of its food on the open market. One irony was that the Ethiopian Orthodox Church, which owns 20 per cent of the arable land in all of Ethiopia, was suspected of speculating on grain prices during the famine. While foreign missionaries and non-Orthodox Ethiopians (especially the Ethiopian Church of Makane Yesus) were at the vanguard of famine relief efforts, the Orthodox Church remained silent. It refused to help, despite the fact that it is the one institution in Ethiopia that reaches into every province, village, and Christian household. Critics charged that the Orthodox Church's lack of temporal concern for the starving was because many of the sufferers were Moslems. Others thought the Church had a predisposition toward the nobility of guilt, suffering, and death—especially with regard to peasants. Still other critics felt the Church remained silent because of its close political ties to the throne, and moreover because it couldn't connect famine relief with conversion to the Orthodox Church.

Whatever the reasons, His Holiness the Patriarch of Ethiopia never spoke out about the famine, and he and his church refused to cooperate on any level with the other religious groups, whom *ipso facto* the Patriarch regarded as arch-rivals.

More than 280,000 refugees, according to Wollo provincial statistics, gathered in the villages along the main highway. They ate weeds and weed seeds. Sister Jutta, a nun working in Alitena, reported: "The people are in great distress." Thor Skubeck of the Swedish Community School drove north to see the situation for himself. "Between Robi and

---

*Injera and Wat is the national dish of Ethiopia, a meal of flat bread and meat gravy. Faffa is a highly concentrated food.

50 kilometers north of there (Sunbutte), children are starving. Mothers were out in the road trying to stop any car that came along. The situation is very bad."

These were the lucky ones. Behind them, in the interior, countless numbers of others unable to walk out to the highway died. Peasants interviewed in the relief centers estimated that deaths in their home villages had reached as many as 20 to 50 per cent of the inhabitants and more.

Provincial officials, ever mindful of IEG distaste, herded the drought victims into hastily erected, makeshift relief camps. Father Doheny found people in Dessie sleeping out in the open. He was told that there were 5,000 people in the small town, and for some unknown reason the feeding program had temporarily shut down. Six thousand people packed into the town of Mersa believing that there was food. There wasn't. The refugee camp at Bati fed 1,000 women and children a day; half the dying were children. Kobbo had 400 children and 200 sickly adults lining up for food one day. Three days later there were 1,000 children.

Alamata had 8,000 refugees, and ten a day died from starvation. Sister Helen, working in Tigre, reported to CRF: "the people still continue to come, some days up to 30 in number. Each new group seems to us to look more ragged, tired, and sick than the former. There are more than 250 people, elderly and women and children, living out of doors." Father Doheny began stuffing the trunks of cars heading north from Addis with drugs and medicines for the relief camps springing up along the Addis-Asmara highway.

Whatever arrived was badly needed. Two Oxfam* representatives visited the camps in Wollo and Tigre and reported: "In nearly all shelters the diet for the malnourished children is deficient in both calories and proteins due to an irregular and inadequate supply of food. To take only one example, we found in one shelter that the only protein being provided to the 205 under-ten-year-old children, whatever their nutritional state, is one-tenth of a litre of milk made up from dried skimmed milk every three days.

"From the figures given to us by the staff at each of the different centers in Wollo, not less than 600 people are dying each week in the ten shelters visited."

---

*Formerly the Oxford Committee for Famine Relief.

Overcrowding in the camps produced ideal conditions for the spread of disease. As the starving-but-well mixed with the starving-and-sick, epidemics started. Smallpox, meningitis, dysentery, pneumonia, typhus, measles (that killed the children) swept the camps.

In June, there was the first outbreak—but not the last—of what the IEG, even in its internal memos from the Ministry of Public Health, insisted be called "gastro-enteritis C." It was a strangely fatal disease. In the town of Assaita, for example, deaths from "gastro-enteritis C" were so numerous that the bodies were stacked in the streets awaiting burial. Foreign relief officials in Wollo and Tigre were ordered to call the disease simply "dysentery" and did so for fear of incurring IEG displeasure.

The minutes of Christian Relief's weekly meetings, however, detailed the spreading sickness. In its field reports, the word dysentery was placed in quotes; CRF pointed out that widespread vaccination programs were urgently needed for "dysentery," and, as careful readers could understand, no one gets vaccinated against such a disease.

July 2nd, 1973—*Report from the Field.*

Medical situation: Bati health centre has "100 patients suffering from Amoebic Dysentery," and 8 per day die from it.

July 9th, 1973—*Report from the Field.*

Tigre: The doctors report that "dysentery" is "making its claims in the area. The government is vaccinating where there are

> outbreaks, but still they are burying five to six people per day." A nearby village, Gouwanni, is suffering ten deaths per day. "Some places tell of nineteen per day and burying two bodies in one grave."

July 16th, 1973—*Report from the Field.*

> *Situation in Bati is very bad. "There is an outbreak of sickness. Some call it [amoebic] dysentery." . . . There are 10,000 in Bati needing help. Five people die daily, and rate is on the increase. The Mission has 250 patients with dysentery. Many have been vaccinated. Need blankets immediately. Many dying from exposure.*

> *Hasaita: "Situation really desperate. Outbreaks of sickness are very serious."*

So began one of the worst stages of the international famine coverup—a shocking example of bureaucratic paralysis and timidity, by both international civil servants and professional diplomats, that directly caused the death of thousands of Ethiopians.

One of the basic questions about the international coverup of Ethiopia's famine is: What allowed this conspiracy of silence to operate? After all, Haile Selassie and the Ethiopian government might *wish* the famine covered up, but that didn't guarantee that it would be. That their request for a conspiracy of silence was honored was the result of, among other things, close relationships between international civil servants, especially at UN agencies, professional diplomats, and the IEG. It was also the result of blind international adherence to the standards of national sovereignty where an unparalleled natural disaster had rendered that sovereignty an empty shell. Haile Selassie, a revered old man, and deservedly so, had become irrelevant and indifferent, or deaf, to the problems of his people. He was the head of a government presiding over a country in chaos. The IEG wasn't dealing realistically with any portion of the disaster they were facing and was no longer a functioning government. To what extreme lengths was it appropriate for the international community to go in its sensitivity toward a government no longer protecting its people? And more directly, should a diplomat protect the reputation of a foreign government regardless of the cost to its people and particularly in circumstances where the outside world retains important leverage? In the case of Ethiopia, honorable men and women working for honorable institutions refused to jeopardize their jobs or their comfortable relationship with Haile Selassie's government by calling international attention to Ethiopia's "secret."

"It is not our job to get publicity," one UN official later told the *Guardian*. "We are an international organization who work under clear rules. We carrry out programs sought and approved by the [Ethiopian] Government." And when that program was one of keeping quiet, the United Nations, too, would remain silent.

Nowhere was this better seen than during one of the events of July and August, 1973, when the value of protecting "working relationships" outweighed the value of human life itself. That event was the outbreak of the "gastro-enteritis C" epidemic. For behind the deaths from "gastro-enteritis C" lay another, almost sinister, coverup, which explained much about how international agencies and the international community work (or don't work) and why such agencies could have gone along with the IEG on the larger issue of covering up the famine.

By early July, 1973, the IEG Ministry of Public Health (MPH), WHO, UNICEF, WFP, FAO, the U.S. Peace Corps, and UNDP knew and held meetings to discuss the fact that "gastro-enteritis C," or "dysentery," was actually cholera.

Word had spread slowly and quietly in Addis, beginning in late June. Two Peace Corps volunteers, in a casual discussion with Stephen Green, a courageous and outspoken UNICEF worker, revealed that cholera was sweeping the drought areas. A WHO doctor who had been traveling in the region confirmed this. So did an American resident doctor in the Seventh Day Adventist Hospital in Addis, who told of widespread deaths in six mission clinics in Wollo and Tigre. Lab tests confirmed the deaths came from cholera. The American doctor offered Stephen Green a ride on a plane flying intravenous fluids to one mission clinic, and Green reported on August 14, 1973, to UNICEF:

"From the air, the dust and drought conditions were horrible. Livestock losses visible from the air were virtually total. The pilot flew us over many villages along half the length of one of the major valleys in Ethiopia, where graveyards had doubled in size in recent months. Virtually all of the graveyards seen showed signs of burials taking place. In Assiata, the site of the mission clinic, the worst was confirmed. Discussions with angry Health Officers revealed the number of deaths. The Director of the MPH Special Cholera Team, however, maintained that he was under strict instructions not to discuss the problem with anyone, least of all with someone from an international organization."

In Addis Ababa, the IEG worried about a quarantine against its exports, embarrassment to itself, or a fall-off of tourism, and instructed the agencies and embassies to be quiet about the cholera. When those with power refused to speak out, those without power were placed in an impossible position. As Father Doheny of Christian Relief stated to the

Guardian, "If the United Nations stays quiet, how can I possibly speak out? If I do, I shall be forced out of the country, and even *our* work will cease." When a foreign missionary nurse in Wollo pleaded with the UN representatives in Addis for help, the IEG Minister of Public Health, Ketema Abebe, personally told her: "We're fully competent to deal with the situation. If you mention the word cholera to one more UN official, you'll be out of the country in forty-eight hours."

IEG competence, however, was questionable. The chief of the IEG's Ministry of Public Health Epidemiology Division confirmed that the MPH was "running dangerously short of intravenous fluids, anti-biotics, supplementary food, and other materials need to combat the lethal combinations of famine and severe gastro-intestinal disorders."

To discuss these problems, the UNDP representative in Addis called a meeting of the concerned international agencies in early August, 1973. During that meeting, several startling facts were established:

- The cholera outbreak was more widespread than previously reported.

- Information on the size and devastation of the cholera epidemic had been relayed to regional offices, including UNICEF's New York headquarters emergency desk. As of August 14, 1973, after thousands of Ethiopians had died from cholera, nothing was being done.

- The Ethiopian Ministry of Public Health was inadequately equipped and staffed to deal with the problem alone and was concentrating its efforts on vaccinations, ineffectual at this late date, rather than massive medical aid.

- The UN agencies, following traditional diplomatic practice, refused to act without a formal request for assistance from the Imperial Ethiopian government—a request they all knew would never come and had, in fact, been denied. An official of the Ministry of Public Health had already told a group of UN workers: "For commercial and political reasons, the government does not want the situation known, and the World Health Organization has been informed that no formal request for assistance will be forthcoming."

- Nor would these UN agencies call attention to the disaster unilaterally—despite their full awareness of the seriousness and scope of the epidemic—because, as they admitted, such action would endanger close and long-term relationships with the Imperial government.

The World Health Organization was especially irresponsible. WHO, with its international communicable disease warning system, was obligated to report the outbreak of cholera. Not only was this disease infecting those Ethiopians in the relief camps but also nomads wandering into the Sudan, Djibouti, Somalia, and Kenya. According to a report of the meeting, WHO, however, was more concerned about maintaining "a good working relationship" with the IEG and was "understandably reluctant to jeopardize a number of delicate negotiations on long-term projects (and, in fact, its very continued existence in the country) in pursuit of a request which, if made and granted, might or might not result in the actual saving of lives.

WHO remained silent. It refused to make public an epidemic spreading across international boundaries. Neither would WHO force the issue with the IEG and thereby threaten "long-term projects," nor would it press the IEG to request assistance. The other agencies also remained silent and justified their inaction with a convenient diplomatic problem: the UNDP representative admitted that he recognized "the seriousness of the situation," as did his advisors from WFP and FAO. But he was "powerless to act without a formal request from the [Imperial] Government." In a perfect "Catch-22," the other UN agencies agreed that something should be done, but that there was the "ticklish issue of pursuing this essentially medical matter without the formal advice of the [the UNDP's] medical advisor"—the WHO representative.

The meeting dissolved into academic questions at a time when immediate action was vital: If the government does not wish assistance, how far can international agencies go to press that assistance on the government?; and, If the request for emergency supplies were made, could UN agencies respond quickly with the kind of assistance needed?

The meeting failed to answer any of these questions. Stephen Green, present with the other UN representatives, despaired: "Tens, perhaps scores, of people are dying daily in Ethiopia for want of simple and inexpensive medical supplies and procedures. Carriers may be crossing daily into countries that are not aware of this problem. Yet the UN system is unable to respond to the situation or even acknowledge its existence."

Indeed, the "UN system" and the international community were going along with a coverup of the very situation international cooperation in technical fields is designed to combat. This conspiracy of silence meant that IEG officials, while denying the existence of cholera in Ethiopia, could sell donated vaccines urgently needed by medical workers in the relief camps. It meant a shortage of fluids to treat the dehydration caused by the disease. And it meant death: without proper treatment, especially intravenous feeding of massive dosages of fluids, 60 per cent of all cholera victims die.*

---

*Cholera spreads when human waste from infected persons contaminates food or water supplies. It generally strikes overcrowded villages or refugee camps. Cholera causes diarrhea and vomiting, and death within six hours. The incubation period is usually about three days or less. Severe dehydration causes death, and treatment includes replacing body fluids and salts in large doses, with as much as a quart of fluids and salts put into a victim's veins in an hour.

As the people died, the officials talked. Both WHO and the IEG admitted informally that basic supplies like intravenous fluids would have saved "many lives." Yet the UN agencies, safeguarding "working relationships" between themselves and the IEG, refused to act. Whether covering up the cholera epidemic or the spreading famine for the Imperial government, the international agencies and donor nations knew what was happening and kept silent.

In fact, as late as July, 1973, some UN agencies still debated whether or not a famine existed in Ethiopia. The World Food Programme said there was a famine. But UNICEF in New York, even when sent cables from Addis Ababa, claimed no knowledge of "a famine" in Ethiopia. When the World Food Programme undertook an investigation of the starvation in July, 1973, its report detailing conditions in Wollo and Tigre was circulated privately within the UN community but was not made public. For one thing, WFP grain supplies were low, mostly concentrated in West Africa. But had that report been publicized, it might have started large-scale relief pouring into Ethiopia six months earlier than it did.

While the United Nations debated, peasants bartered for food by trading clothing given them by missionaries. Others ate animal feed. By late July, the rains fell, too late and too strong to help. Pneumonia swept the relief camps. Dirt roads, which had proven woefully inadequate for the distribution of relief supplies during the dry season, became impassable. In Dessie, the police reported that drought victims lying in the streets in the rain were too weak to raise their heads and drowned.

VI

No longer was the famine a secret. By mid-August, 1973, the international agencies and the donor nations had complete knowledge of its scale and severity. Yet only Christian Relief, which made widely available the minutes of its meetings, spoke openly:

August 6th, 1973—*Report from the Field.*

The Tigre Relief Fund purchased grain in Asmara and paid all transportation costs. There are 60,000 starving people in the area, "and they are suffering intensely, the children in particular." Most of the livestock died in Wajara and the farmers now plow with hoes.

10,000 in Bati, and 15 per day dying of starvation at the relief center . . . Farmers eating seeds in Werababu . . . The Governor of Tigre claims that 50 Danakils in the province are dying daily of famine. "They have grain, but no means of getting it to the Danakil region."

"Enormous numbers of cattle" owned by the Danakils "can be seen dying by the roadside daily." . . . Danakils suffering. "Vultures and hyenas . . . ate up the carcasses."

August 13th, 1973—*Report from the Field.*

Kombolcha: ". . . tin houses built accommodating 200-300 people, but there is only mud for the people to lie on . . .

Rations are insufficient, but the government [is] only able to give this amount as stocks are small. We were told by the meat factory workers that up to 100 poor people come every evening, and if cattle have died outside the gates, these people remove any meat and eat it there and then."

Hausa: On the morning of August 10th, 750 people lined up for food, and 79 were children; 40 others were "unable to walk from the tin houses to collect their food, due to extreme weakness."

Kobbo: 400 died last month. Bati is feeding 500.

August 20th, 1973—*Report from the Field.*

". . . The situation in Mersa [is] very sad and distressing. The floods had caused great devastation and their first work was to dig out bodies from the debris, and bury them. About 36 were buried on August the 15th, the first day. One child was clinging to the mother not realising she was dead. Another child was so bad that he was taken as dead, and was found to be alive later."

At Dessie, 1,900 people lie around the center waiting care; 150 new arrivals every day.

Kobbo: 1,000 "destitute people" being fed. "The death-rate is very high. In the orphanage, catering for 135 children, 27 have died in the past month. At present there are five cases of 'dysentery.'" In the Awash Valley there are 28,600 people "in desperate need."

August 27th, 1973—*Report from the Field.*

Thirteen plane-loads of food flown into the Danakil; 50 tons, mostly bags of corn, dropped by air to help feed 30,000 people. "At present it is impossible to reach Zobel, Lastra and Wadja." Food-for-Work programme now includes grave digging. "One man employed as a grave digger missed his wife, but later recognized her at the grave yard. She had died of starvation."

UNICEF sent a two-man team into Wollo in late August, 1973. Their report detailed the full seriousness of the famine and placed the deaths from starvation between 50,000 and 100,000 people. The UNICEF report further stated that 283,000 starving peasants in Wollo—out of 670,000 people who were hungry and needing food in the province—had registered at relief centers along the Addis-Asmara highway and had received some food and grain supplies.*

The report privately elicited shocked denials from the Ethiopian government, which sought to limit its circulation as narrowly as possible. One IEG minister told UNICEF coldly: "If it is a choice between making this public and not receiving aid, then we can do without the aid."

UNICEF circulated its report among the various international agencies in Addis, but insisted that it be kept quiet. "It was clear to everyone that its contents were not to be divulged," said one UNICEF official. The IEG privately called the report "a grotesque exaggeration." (To publicly denounce it would have required an explanation of what the report contained.) The UNICEF chief in Addis Ababa thought the report was accurate. "But the head of UNICEF in Geneva thought the statistics were unreliable," said a U.S. embassy officer in Addis. "The donors buried it."

USAID, for one, passed the UNICEF report on to Washington with the IEG's denunciation but without any evaluation or criticism of that denunciation. In Washington, USAID's failure to comment was read as an endorsement of the IEG's attack. But senior U.S. government officials in Addis and Washington knew full well that there were a lot of Ethiopians starving to death and that the drought was far more severe than the IEG privately admitted. After all, they had seen the cable reports from their own junior staff members in June and July. "There was a conspiracy of silence all along the line—the IEG, UNICEF, USAID, WHO," said a U.S. embassy official. At least three U.S. embassy workers in Addis Ababa questioned USAID about why they thought the UNICEF figures were inflated. USAID replied, "Because the IEG did."

As early as July, Stephen Green, then newly appointed to work with UNICEF's two-man office in Ethiopia and a member of the team that put together UNICEF's report, told the Christian Relief Fund committee that the United Nations was awaiting a formal request for aid from the IEG. After UNICEF's report was made, however, Mitiku Jembere, Ethiopia's vice-minister of planning, scolded: "Let me put it this way; if we have to describe the situation the way you have in your report in order to generate international assistance, then we don't want that assistance. The embarrassment to the government isn't worth it. Is that perfectly clear?"

---

*An unpublished IEG report later calculated that by the end of August there were 284,000 people getting aid in Wollo, but the number starving, based on reports from the *awraja* governors, was 840,000. In Tigre, 322,000 were starving, including 96,600 children, according to figures at the relief camps. How many went uncounted in the interior is unknown.

Indeed it was. IEG officials would rather let Ethiopians starve than have the government embarrassed.

But the UNICEF report was leaked to a London newspaper, and European journalists began appearing in Addis Ababa for a first-hand look. Among them, Jonathan Dimbleby, a British television documentary producer, entered Ethiopia at the end of September. The minister of information, after a heated cabinet discussion, agreed to let Dimbleby in, and the reporter convinced the IEG to allow him to film some of "the problem of drought." He was finally able to look at a few of the best relief camps along the highway in Wollo.

That was enough. Dimbleby took his film back to England. The IEG knew the cat, at last, was out of the bag. The IEG flew an official to London to get Dimbleby to "tone down the film." Dimbleby refused. When the film was shown, the IEG sent a note to all embassies in London accusing Dimbleby of "distortion and exaggeration." Dimbleby's stirring documentary shocked Europeans in the fall of 1973, and contributions to Oxfam, the Lutheran World Federation, the British Save the Children Fund, and other agencies flooded in. When *Stern*, the German magazine, also published an account of the famine, it too was swamped with contributions. *Stern* set up a special fund for relief aid to Ethiopia and by March, 1974, had pumped in more tangible famine aid than most donor nations, including the United States.*

Diseases continued sweeping the camps. The CRF reports came in. In Bati, 1,700 people had cholera, and 12 to 14 died every day. Kombolcha had 1,000 inside the relief center, mainly women, children, and the elderly, and "the number of patients is increasing daily and further medicines are needed urgently. The death rate is increasing." Malaria and pneumonia struck in the Awash Valley shelters. Asaito listed 7,000 people "in great need." In Weldiya, 800 people crowded into fifteen "rooms" and "conditions are very poor." Some 600 others outside the shelter were being fed whatever was left over after those inside the shelter had eaten. Some 500 people were being fed in Wegessa, and perhaps 20 died every day. At Kobbo, 1,500 crowded into the shelters, and smallpox, measles, "and now typhus," ravaged them. Dr. H. Ypma reported to the CRF committee: "Contagious diseases are rife and there is a lack of correct diagnosis and medicines."

---

*The United States, according to a March, 1974, report, had only donated a small amount of what it had pledged: 4,040 tons of grain (versus 33,000 tons pledged); $5,000 out of the ambassador's $25,000 Emergency Fund (donated to Christian Relief); one public health specialist; and $1,027.29 donated to Ethiopian World Federation. It was, said one private relief agency worker, "incredible—a pittance."

Dessie had 600 cases of typhoid on record in September, and relief workers were able to treat only "the worst cases among the children." On September 24, 1973, for example, there were 3,976 patients at Dessie and 338 children "needing urgent attention." The camp was prepared to treat five cases a day, "but because of the need we are now expanding to make 60 beds available—4 to a bed. Many arrive unconscious and are therefore difficult to feed." In some ways, the camps were actually worse than the villages left behind. In Dessie: "hygenic conditions in the camp are deplorable, with swarms of flies everywhere. Dysentery is very common and something must be done at once to improve the hygenic conditions of the compound—latrines, etc., must be built." What few latrines they did have "could do with some lime at least to discourage the flies."

The IEG-supervised relief camps were a disaster. In a secret report to the IEG cabinet in November, 1973, twelve Ethiopian officials said that the camps were so bad they caused unnecessary deaths. The report added: "Due to poor care and administration, especially at night, the shelters are littered with feces and urine and sometimes dead bodies." An Ethiopian doctor who inspected the Wollo camps in November wrote of "inhuman conditions." If reports that the camps have improved are true, he said, "things must have been intolerable before." The camps were characterized by "organizational chaos and shortsightedness."

In fact, conditions in the relief camps reflected a deeper problem. There was little coordination between the IEG and the Christian Relief Fund. As the number of peasants needing help increased, the ability of the missionaries and volunteers to care for them diminished. They were too few and the starving too many. One volunteer said: "The relief operation is a shambles." Another volunteer called the lack of coordination between the IEG and church agencies "appalling." The CRF, at its October 1, 1973, meeting, passed a resolution "to express in the strongest possible terms the need and absolute necessity for greater cooperation between [the] churches and government agencies, Red Cross, UN, etc. so that the confusion now existing in the field might be reduced and if possible eliminated."

For one thing, very little food had arrived in the country; most was purchased in the commercial markets. The total amount of grain *delivered* to Wollo and Tigre by IEG, church, and private sources, including donor nations, between May and August, 1973—in the middle of a famine that hardened relief workers described as worse than Biafra—was just 1,400 tons. At Kobbo, supplies of food were low and expected IEG grain didn't come. In Wuchale, the army tried to distribute what little food was available, but so many starving people flocked in that they blocked the roads. Stephen Green and Tiruneh Sinnshaw wrote this vivid description in their UNICEF report at the end of August, 1973:

"We need not wonder what would happen to the large concentrations of people at the distribution points should the feeding suddenly cease—it has happened already. Six weeks ago shortages caused the sudden cessation of feeding in Dessie at a time when over 10,000 were registered and receiving food. The margin of strength of those suddenly told to return to their villages was simply not great enough. The bodies of some were found partially eaten by hyenas on both the roads to Haik and Kombolcha."

The IEG, and some international agencies, wanted the peasants sent back to their villages as soon as possible. Perhaps the IEG, for one, found the presence of large groups of hungry, restless peasants uncomfortable. It was also embarrassing: after all, a starving or dying peasant represented tangible proof to television cameras and nosey reporters of official failure or indifference. By sending the peasants back, moreover, it was hoped that they might help with the December harvest and thereby ease the famine.

In Wollo particularly, the peasants were sent out of the camps.* In early October, Kombolcha sent away 20 a day who were fit. Some 150 a day moved away from the Dessie camp after getting food and grain to start them off. More than 1,000 went off from Weldiya, and the government encouraged them with grain and transport.

It didn't work. For one thing, as Stephen Green and Tiruneh Sinnshaw made clear, the peasants weren't strong enough to hike back to their deserted villages. They had no plow oxen, no seed, and little hope. One report to CRF emphasized: "The relief programs must continue for a long time." Ethiopia's peasants needed too much before they could recover. In the words of one volunteer: "There is not enough aid, and aid is not enough." The Reverend G. Jabs of the Ethiopian Church of Makane Yesus told CRF that the relief camps were a long-term necessity: "We cannot move out to the people, and many are dying. Mountains make the countryside inaccessible, and people spend ten hours coming out to the main road when they are well. Now, when they are starving, it takes them three or four days to drag themselves out . . . . The camps are therefore necessary to keep the people alive."

---

*In Tigre, where Ras Mengasha Seyoum had built feeder roads, many peasants could stay in their villages and get fed. Ras Mengasha also commandeered a DC-3 for airdrops. "His impact on the drought," said a diplomat, "was substantial." Still, said one survey in 1973, Tigre suffered "serious shortages" and "food prospects for 1974 are gloomy."

VII

For weeks during the late fall of 1973, British and European journalists reported the famine conditions in Ethiopia. Dimbleby's documentary of the victims horrified an international audience and alerted the international press, up to that point ignorant of the major human drama unfolding. The worldwide relief effort geared up. But the IEG fought the publicity. In Addis Ababa, incoming magazines and newspapers were censored and reached subscribers with articles carefully snipped out or entire pages missing. Some were banned entirely. There was no famine in Ethiopia unless the Imperial Ethiopian government said there was, and the IEG refused to admit what the world was already beginning to learn in shocking detail.

In October, 1973, for example, Dr. Mehari Gebre-Medhin, acting director of the Ethiopian Nutrition Institute, told an official of the Swedish International Development Authority (SIDA): "We've always had localized food shortages in Ethiopia. This is nothing new. The only difference now is that a lot of foreigners know about it and are getting excited." At this same time, the Ethiopian Nutrition Institute was preparing a report, not made public until April, 1974, showing that one in five Ethiopians had died in Wollo Province in 1973 and that the total number who would starve to death might reach 500,000 there alone.*

---

*Accurate death totals may never be compiled. It is clear, however, from reading reports and minutes of meetings during 1973 and 1974 that the scale of suffering

As the publicity spread, supplies increased. The IEG's effort to fight the publicity was reduced to harassment. Two badly needed Christian Relief Fund Land Rovers that could carry food to the interior were delayed several weeks because the IEG wanted customs paid on the donated vehicles. Two tons of Oxfam blankets were held up at one port because the relief agency didn't have certificates showing that they had been fumigated—a strange necessity considering their destination. CRF members got their donated trucks shipped to Ethiopian ports, only to begin long discussions with IEG bureaucrats over who would pay for the gasoline.

The IEG was buying time. It hoped that the December harvest would be large enough to get it off the hook and encourage peasants to return to their villages and land. But a Ministry of Agriculture crop survey showed that the harvests in Wollo and Tigre would be inadequate. Indeed, the Ministry of Agriculture, a year after its first warning, issued another: vast areas of *southern* Ethiopia would suffer nearly total crop failures, and the number of Ethiopians affected by drought might double in 1974.

"It is now generally known," said the Ministry's report, "that a severe drought has been prevailing . . . reaching famine proportions in 1973. It is now obvious that the numbers of people affected by the drought are much higher than hitherto provided for and that a much more intense relief operation will have to be undertaken if the peoples of the region are to survive."

Despite the Ministry of Agriculture's second warning in a year, Haile Selassie announced in November during his Speech from the Throne that "the problem of drought" was "being satisfactorily tackled through food and medical relief organizations through a Nationwide and Private Crusade."

Two other reports, however, quickly shattered that illusion. One was an IEG report, called "The Drought Problem in Ethiopia," that was circulated to the international agencies and foreign embassies in Addis Ababa on November 15, 1973. The IEG was surprisingly candid in this report after months of denial. The drought was called "unprecedented";

---

was understated and unreported. Small accounts give details of the immensity. One day in the fall of 1973, for example, a foreign relief worker driving along a twelve-mile stretch of the Addis-Asmara road counted 179 bodies. A church group found everyone in a remote village of 62 dead. In the El Kere *awraja*, all 1,477 people died from the famine. A church mission group made a survey of the Kambata *awraja* of southern Shoa Province and found that 11,281 people had died from starvation in 1973, "and that was not even supposed to be a famine area."

its "causes may go beyond the mere fact of the failure of rains to come at their usual time and in their usual quantity." The report placed Ethiopia's crop loss at between 75 and 80 per cent of the normal harvest. It estimated that half the cattle died in the highlands and 90 per cent among the nomads. Moreover, 60 per cent of the arable land in Tigre and Wollo hadn't been planted during the long-rains season.

The drought's impact on the people was equally shocking. The IEG, carefully taking statistics from registrations at relief camps and interviewing *awraja* governors, estimated that in five provinces—Tigre, Wollo, Shoa, Harrarghe, Begemdir, and Gemu Gofa—some 1,098,300 adults and 470,700 children were starving. That is, almost 8 per cent of Ethiopia's people were suffering from famine.

The IEG report, in many facts, corroborated another report that had appeared earlier in the fall. The UN Development Programme had reviewed the situation inside Ethiopia through September 30, 1973. The UNDP report, relying on IEG data supplemented by first-hand field reports, measured the effect of the famine on the Ethiopian people themselves and stated: "It must be reported that the impact of the famine on the physical condition of the population has been general and severe. Estimates of deaths number in the tens of thousands, and, in relief camps and shelters, over 100,000 people are living in conditions inimical to the preservation of a reasonable standard of health. The health conditions of persons without access to camps and health facilities can only be surmised. The availability of medical care within the camps is uneven; some camps have no qualified resident medical personnel, and where such personnel are available they are inadequate in number and inadequately supplied and equipped. . . ."

UNDP had also measured the impact of the drought upon the land. The drought affected, said its report, ". . . the quality of land under cultivation, the yields from crops which have been planted, the amount of water forage and grazing available for livestock, and thus the condition of the human and livestock populations of the region." The result was ". . . debilitation and decimation of livestock. . . . For the nomadic populations (about 125,000 people) . . . the effects have been catastrophic, making the nomads almost totally dependent on food relief . . . ."

The publicity generated by both reports exposed for the world the IEG coverup; for the few who paid attention, it also revealed the underlying collusion by the international community in that coverup. New accusations quickly followed, for both the UNDP report and the IEG survey enumerated the total failure of the international relief community to supply anything near what Ethiopia needed.

In April, 1973, the Ministry of Agriculture had placed the demand at 60,000 metric tons of grain to replace failed harvests. Relief workers in the field estimated that another 9,000 tons a month would be needed to halt starvation. These contacts with the international community elicited pledges that by November, 1973, had reached just 40,000 metric tons—less than the amount needed for five months. And of that 40,000 metric tons, the United States had pledged 22,500.

But for all the international community might pledge, it delivered little. In its November, 1973, report, the IEG claimed that it had received $637,158.03 in cash donations, 319,450 kilograms of milk, milk powder, or other baby food—and just 4,469 metric tons of grain.

The UNDP had listed and the IEG report updated the tally of pledges and what had actually arrived by early November, 1973. It was a meager bag:

• The Swedish International Development Authority—with a solid reputation for flexibility in disaster situations—had only diverted seed grains from existing agricultural projects already inside Ethiopia.

• Great Britain had provided $62,700 for Food-for-Work projects. Oxfam also kicked in $37,500 with Great Britain and, in fact, had promised assistance to the Christian Relief Fund as early as May, although an Oxfam medical team of nine didn't arrive until October in the Dessie and Kombolcha relief camps.

• The Federal Republic of Germany was paying for the transport of grain to the provinces and had promised DM. 500,000 for purchasing trucks.

• The Swiss were just then making available 20 tons of milk powder, 600,000 water purification tablets, 3,000 blankets, and $5,000.

• The International Red Cross had promised 120 tons of milk powder and delivered 75 tons of wheat flour through the Ethiopian Red Cross.

• The European Economic Community had made an "official commitment" of only 5,000 tons of grain. The IEG report said, "It is hoped that additional assistance will be considered by the Community in the near future."

• UNICEF—which played a major role in Biafra and Bangladesh—had only diverted 52,000 pounds of skim milk powder and 315,000 pounds of corn-soy-milk already in Ethiopia under existing programs.

USAID and WFP had been asked in April for the largest amount of aid and had responded with two major pledges. USAID, however, only diverted 2,000 metric tons of grain already in Ethiopia from its Food-for-Work programs. By early November, 1973, not a bag of its 8,000-metric-ton pledge had arrived. WFP, having been asked for 20,000 metric tons in April, pledged 10,000 in May (5,000 of wheat, 2,500 each of corn and sorghum). By October, none of its 10,000-metric-ton pledge had arrived in Ethiopia, either. Worse, the WFP was only then *studying* the question of providing the balance of the 20,000 metric tons requested.

But where the international agencies and major donors had acted slowly, two nations came quickly to Ethiopia's aid. Kenya, already feeling the impact of increasing drought in her own farm lands, delivered in November, 1973, some 10,000 metric tons of maize and another ten tons of powdered milk. During that same month, the People's Republic of China pledged, shipped to Ethiopia, and delivered 10,000 metric tons of grain.*

But even this grain wasn't enough. The drought, as the Ministry of Agriculture pointed out, was spreading southward and engulfing greater numbers of peasants and nomads. The UNDP report called for more relief supplies and warned: "Food aid will be required through 1974 to meet the minimum requirements of the Provinces of Wollo and Tigre in excess of their anticipated production, in an amount of about 150,000 tons of grain."

The IEG report, moreover, made a darker projection. It estimated that the average Ethiopian consumes twenty kilograms of grain per adult per month and the average Ethiopian child eats five kilograms per child per month. From this it concluded that there were 1,569,000 *starving* Ethiopians in five provinces and they would need in 1974 some 268,800 metric tons of grain and 28,800 tons of milk or milk powder to stay alive.

Obviously, the need far surpassed the pledges. UNDP scolded the reluctant donors, especially the WFP. "In the opinion of this office," the UNDP report concluded, "this Assessment makes a clear and compelling case for the World Food Program to provide the second 10,000 tons *tranche* of grain of the 20,000 tons requested from WFP by the IEG in May, 1973, and demonstrates that the requirement is urgent."

Strangely, officials at the U.S. State Department persisted during the fall in giving "optimistic assessments" to congressional staff members inquiring about famine conditions in Ethiopia.** Donald S. Brown

---

*The IEG included an explicit disclaimer in its report admitting that "the above list is far from complete and there are a number of other donors who are actively participating in the relief programme. . . ." But in fact, even such vitally needed programs as in-country *faffa* production and water supply exploration were only in the early planning stages by the time of the report's appearance.

**Optimism—and myopia—pervaded the United States government. In the late summer of 1973, Maurice Williams, the Nixon administration's special presidential relief coordinator, told the President that "mass famine—which

deputy assistant administrator, Bureau of Africa, USAID, would later explain that USAID was busy making "successive approximations" of the situation in Tigre and Wollo, approximations that consistently underestimated Ethiopia's relief needs for 1974. USAID guessed at up to 80,000 metric tons; the total need, however, would soon reach 168,000 metric tons.

Worse, while the UNDP officials now spoke openly of the "serious" famine conditions in Ethiopia, the U.S. ambassador in Addis, former Republican Congressman E. Ross Adair, had not bothered to discuss with IEG officials any major aspect of the famine or the coverup or to declare an emergency—or cable for urgent relief supplies. Any U.S. ambassador may request and receive $25,000 from the Special Ambassador's Fund for discretionary use in emergencies. Further, a declaration of emergency from a U.S. ambassador clears internal U.S. bureaucratic channels and opens channels for broader and more immediate U.S. government assistance. While the question of a nation's sovereignty is delicate (and relevant) here, other U.S. ambassadors have acted quickly under conditions similar to those facing Ambassador Adair.*

But while his staff visited the relief camps, attended UN and embassy meetings about the drought and famine, and filed emotional and detailed cables to Washington, Ambassador Adair, a political appointee of the Nixon administration, delayed. Like others in Addis Ababa, he waited for a formal request for assistance from the IEG. And like others in the Ethiopian capital, Ambassador Adair knew the IEG wouldn't make such a formal request unless pressured.

Fortunately, the growing publicity and the two reports were providing some pressure. The reports were soon followed by the traditional Ethiopian method of expressing concern—an imperial visit. From November 27 to 29, Haile Selassie toured Wollo at the head of a forty-vehicle motorcade. He announced that he was "greatly saddened by the hardship and suffering of our people" and issued some official decrees, among them that land bought from desperate peasants be sold back at the original price, plus interest. (The mechanism for doing this was never described and the imperial order never implemented.) The famine in Ethiopia was now official. Four days later, on December 3, 1973, Am-

---

threatened millions some weeks ago—has been averted." And on March 19, 1974, President Nixon himself told an audience in Houston, Texas: "All over the world people are eating a little better."

*In 1974, although the government of Tanzania had not declared an emergency and was in fact keeping its starvation quiet, the U.S. ambassador in Tanzania started relief aid rolling into the country during its politically sensitive drought.

bassador Adair proclaimed a state of emergency in Ethiopia—eight full months after the IEG had asked his staff for relief aid and six full months after young officers in his embassy had alerted Washington to the disaster.

On November 26, Senator Edward Kennedy wrote to Secretary of State Henry Kissinger about the contrasts between the UNDP report of Ethiopia's food situation and the "optimistic views of officials of our government . . . . If the UNDP report and others are correct in their assessment of the current situation," Senator Kennedy told the secretary of state, "serious questions must be raised as to the adequacy of our government's response . . . . Up to 150,000 tons of food assistance will be needed in 1974, according to the United Nations, just to meet minimum food requirements. Less than 40,000 tons have been committed to date. Despite the recognition last June by USAID that emergency food would be required in Ethiopia on an urgent basis, less than 5,000 tons have arrived.* Only 23,000 tons have been committed by the United States for the coming year . . . . The international community can no longer speak of foreign aid for development, but for mere survival."

During Senate hearings in March, 1974, investigating the worldwide problem of food and drought, Senator Kennedy pursued the question of the slow United States government response to Ethiopia.

"Well, it seems to me, in reviewing the record of this past year," he told Donald Brown of USAID, "we knew about the growing famine conditions in the spring of last year [1973] and we had very little reaction to it. And then after the United Nations report and after our letter, you still gave really a low estimate of the problem; now we find the estimate was about a fourth or a third of what is generally recognized as needed in the whole country.

"It just distresses me about why we are not out in the forefront in recognizing food problems, or pressing this issue forward rather than having to be dragged into it."

Brown denied that USAID or the State Department had been "dragged" into famine relief and argued that they had been in the "forefront" as much as anyone in recognizing the problem. Still, he admitted, ". . . there has been generally slow recognition of the problems because

---

*In fact, according to a letter from the State Department on December 12, 1973, the first U.S. shipment of 4,000 metric tons (of the 22,500-metric-ton pledge) was just then arriving at Ethiopia's ports. The first of the 10,000 metric tons donated by the U.S. government through the World Food Program arrived in late December, and the remainder didn't come into Ethiopia until January, 1974—eight months after it was pledged.

of exceptional difficulty in being able to assess problems, needs in very remote areas."

Brown didn't mention the embassy cables in the spring of 1973 describing the famine. Nor did he reveal that lower levels of the U.S. government had been in the forefront, but that in the U.S. government (as in others) a problem does not exist until it is recognized at the top. Brown also did not reveal that Parker Wyman, deputy chief of mission, had filed a highly detailed letter to the State Department on August 15, 1973. Instead, Brown cited the needs for food in Wollo and Tigre for 1974 and explained that ". . . in the meantime, the problems of the South developed. They . . . are apparently, as far as we can see, spreading rapidly and becoming very difficult. Nobody at this point has a meaningful assessment of what full requirements for the problems in southern Ethiopia will be . . . ."

But Senator Kennedy persisted: "Is not the real reason for our slow response that we just did not want to blow the whistle on the Ethiopian Government? Is that not really the bottom line of it? Perhaps you cannot say it, but that seems to me to be the bottom line. We just did not want to embarrass them, for political reasons. We did not want to expose it. We were not prepared to blow the whistle on it because of our relations with them. As a result, a lot of people starved to death."

Brown implicated the international agencies and other donor nations along with the United States government. Both, he testified, had tried to "bring the Ethiopian Government to greater recognition. We tried to do this in ways that would lead to cooperation and willingness by the Ethiopian Government to take steps on its own . . . ."

But no donor pushed the IEG, or told the Emperor what was happening, or broke the conspiracy of silence. They would not embarrass the Emperor or jeopardize established working relationships.

Brown continued: " . . . there was [a] feeling among many of the donor groups that *raising this to too public an issue, embarrassing the government*, could in fact harm the kind of cooperation we see as needed on their part. In that sense, perhaps the whistle was not blown loudly enough." (Italics added.)

If at all.

Meanhile, the starving continued. Unless there were outstanding harvests, shortages would continue into 1975. Water was at a premium: thirteen relief camps along the Addis-Asmara highway needed water wells. In Sardo, where 3,000 Danakils crowded together in a feeding station, the well was broken; clean water was an hour's walk away.

CRF reports from the field told that water at Weldiya was drawn from a "polluted" well outside the compound; "the tap with a supply of clean water is reserved for the Government Clinic." By December, 1,700 people pressed into the camp at Kombolcha; new arrivals slept out-of-doors. In an area six hours by mule from Mersa, some 1,700 of the 6,000 people living there had alrady starved to death, and "the grain will last only another 3-4 weeks . . . ." The refugees at Bati increased to 2,013, with 80 children orphaned when their parents died in the shelters. Perhaps as many as 3,000 abandoned children roamed Wollo, Tigre, and Shoa provinces.

And the drought was spreading southward. As Donald Brown saw it: "The drama in Ethiopia is still unfolding."

In 1974, as the drought spread southward, destroying land and people, the double coverup was replaced by corruption and bureaucratic bungling. And although aid supplies began arriving, the tragedies of drought and famine got ignored for the high-politics of revolution, secession, and regional big-power strategies.

The drought and famine were unfortunate constants in a land of increasing variables. The tragedy had begun under a conservative government and continued during the radical. It had been there last year and would be there next. In one way or another, the drought and famine touched the lives of every Ethiopian.

At any time between 1973-75, perhaps 8 per cent of the Ethiopian population was starving to death. The number of people perpetually hungry continues at about twenty million. The drought permanently changed the quality of land under cultivation, crop yields, water forage, and grazing. It decimated livestock herds. The widespread hunger created masses of people near death and in various stages of dependency. A survey of Harrarghe Province, for example, revealed ". . . a serious alteration in the life style of the people as a result of the drought."

The needs are staggering: resettlement of masses of people to less populated areas; water, roads, fresh livestock, plow oxen, seed; a change in land tenure and taxation; grain storage and better marketing; water and soil conservation; reforestation; vaccination programs; health clinics; and on, and on.

The social and ecological changes that have taken place mean that

Ethiopia will need assistance from outside for years, perhaps decades. The drought, then, has raised a fundamental question: Can Ethiopia, in the face of recent setbacks, ever receive adequate assistance to become self-sufficient? The answer, given current relations between the developed and developing worlds, may well be no. Then, one must ask: To whom is Ethiopia, after all, important enough to warrant expensive, long-term aid? And what would such dependency mean for the stability in the Horn?

The answers to these questions affect not Ethiopia alone but a host of impoverished states that may be pushed to the edge of mass starvation in the years of scarcity ahead.

By early 1974, missionaries were reporting large pockets of starving people, especially nomads, in the provinces of Harrarghe, Bale, Sidamo, and Gemu Gofa in the south. Near the Kenyan border, one mission reported 5,000 people "in trouble" and cattle dying "in great numbers." The Southern Ethiopian Synod of the Makane Yesus Church stated: "The farmers need substantial help, since *no crops* can be harvested after these [short] rains . . . ." The mission distributed grain to 8,555 families and said that another 7,000 families needed food immediately. The pattern of Wollo and Tigre began to repeat itself: the rains failed, few crops were harvested, and grass-growth was minimal. The peasant farmers ". . . have eaten their seed, and now they are selling their few heads of cattle and oxen, tools and gear, even houses and fields, buying grain to sustain their lives."

In an area covering southern Sidamo and Gemu Gofa, about 860 kilometers by 300 kilometers, 200,000 people were starving. The patterns seen in Wollo and Tigre a year earlier were repeated. In Konso, a tribal unit in southeast Gemu Gofa with a population of 80,000 in two hundred villages, the rains didn't come. ". . . In the village of Wolanta," CRF learned, "from approximately 200 families, only 7 families have grain." Konso men began leaving their homes for Arba Minch, Shelle, Wollamo. "From the village Buso, 300 men have left and 325 from Gadima," leaving the women, children, and old people behind. "Those who have got work either send money home or they buy grain and bring it home, carrying it on their shoulders for as much as three days, and then return to work again." The leader of the government development agency in Konso reported that "the government had started an investigation into the famine problems in Konso. So far no aid has been given."

The Makane Yesus Church warned in 1974, as it had in 1973, of the spreading drought in Kambata, another tribal area:

> In the southeast especially there has been a water problem for some time. The small wells and rivers have dried up and people have begun to walk very long distances to find water. They often walk a whole day with their cattle to a source of water. The calves are too young to do this, so have died or been slaughtered. This drought is now spreading to the Western area.
>
> There is only one health center in the *awraja* and three or four health stations. People suffer a great deal from a kind of dysentery or typhoid, and many have died as a result. Since the report was made many houses . . . have been deserted because some of the inhabitants had died, and others left in the hope of finding a means of survival.
>
> Unless some assistance is given quickly, a large number of people will die. Kambata is the most populated *awraja* in the whole country, with over 800,000 people. . . .*

News of the spreading drought in the south and of 100,000 deaths in Wollo and Tigre sparked an already growing political revulsion inside Ethiopia. A committee at Haile Selassie University reported that "people are starving, sick and dying daily in these hunger-stricken areas." As in Chad, Ethiopian dissidents used the drought and famine to attack an indifferent central government. Ethiopian student groups overseas printed details of the famine and belabored the Selassie government. The Eritrean Liberation Front, from safe positions in Beirut, attacked the IEG as "feudal and corrupt."

March, 1974—*Report from the Field.*

> *Bale . . . area from the River Welmel towards El Kere affected by famine. Prices for cereals are very high and the people are forced to sell cattle cheaply. "They are reported to be cooking leaves to survive."*
>
> *. . . Radio Voice of the Gospel claims that 60 per cent of the cattle have died in the South, leaving the nomads in a "desperate situation." UNDP reports that there are 340,000 people affected by drought in the South and "this is generally considered to be a very low estimate."*
>
> *Tsetse is killing cattle in Gemu Gofa. In Goble, the population of a relief camp doubled "in the last fortnight. The people*

---

*From the March 4, 1974 minutes of the Meeting of the Ad Hoc Committee of the Christian Relief Committee, Addis Ababa.

> *coming in are hungry, but not sick." . . . The water is still bad and it is being carried 7 km partly by women, donkeys and Land Rovers. A well is being drilled by the government, but progress is slow . . . A spring at Burka, population 500, is used by 8,000 people. It is drying up, and the water is muddy and "polluted." The peasants are digging roots for food. One of the village elders from Godabro, Mega District, tells the missionaries his people are scavenging in the woods for roots and edible weeds: "We live just like the baboons."*

The thrust of events and the international community's disarray militated against any coordinated and thorough drought relief program. The drought, with its impact on inflationary urban food prices, its refugees, its social dislocations, and its horror, led to disorders in January, February, and March, 1974. The crisis had an essentially economic impact in the urban areas and prepared the trade unions for militant action. Eventually, bus and taxi drivers, rail and dock workers, police and sanitation men, teachers, bank and airline employees all went out on strike. The upheaval focused attention on the underlying discontent with Ethiopia's archaic social and political system.

Prime Minister Aklilu Habte Wold resigned on February 27, 1974. The army later arrested him. The Ethiopian press, given momentary freedom (freedom which is now at an end), attacked the Aklilu Habte Wold government for suppressing reports of the drought for political reasons. During this "hundred flowers" period, the *Ethiopian Herald,* an English-language daily, charged that "without the inaction of the former government the disaster would never have reached such proportions in Ethiopia."

Endalkachew Makonnen, the next prime minister, pledged greater priority to famine relief. He created a second Relief and Rehabilitation Commission and appointed Ato Shimelis Adugna, former director of prisons and vice-minister of the interior, as its commissioner. The matter of drought would be given the highest priority, Ato Shimelis was told, and the Ethiopian government was at his command for work and aid. In April, Prime Minister Endalkachew placed the Relief and Rehabilitation Commission at Cabinet level, and Ato Shimelis reported directly to him. By mid-June, 1974, the Commission had more than thirty staff members and several foreign experts, plus a cluster of Peace Corps volunteers, working for it.

But the drought was moving faster than the new Ethiopian government. In April, 1974, Haile Selassie University students publicly demanded that the Endalkachew government declare a national state of emergency to deal with the famine in southern Ethiopia. As conditions worsened in the provinces, refugees actually camped on the Parliament grounds in Addis Ababa. On April 15, the IEG sent a busload of them back to the relief camp at Dessie in Wollo. But the drought had come home, and the capital's residents flocked to see and, in some cases, feed the petitioners. The Commission grandly announced that it would purchase 50,000 metric tons of grain for donation to the drought areas. None was ever purchased.

News of the mass starvation, and the IEG's efforts to do something, had finally stimulated international relief. Legions of volunteers—doctors, nurses, engineers, the well-meaning, the concerned— filled the hotels in Addis Ababa. West Germany mounted the most visible early display with radio communications, transport planes flying in tons of food and relief supplies, helicopters whirring into remote areas, and shiny medical relief camps in the desert that looked like extraterrestrial settlements. Ethiopian officials gaped at the growing assortment of disaster relief paraphernalia and struggled to deploy all of it according to a plan that didn't exist.

Wollo and Tigre were now the "popular provinces," largely because the disaster was under control there and the peasants, for the most part, were conveniently clustered at easily reached feeding stations. In Wollo alone, there were forty foreign relief agencies at work by April, 1974. Few relief workers wanted to go south, however, where conditions were harsh and the drought, which swept into Somalia in early 1975, was just beginning. There were few feeding stations in the south, and once again the missionaries carried the burden.

In effect, the nomads were discriminated against. Unless they sought help, few would be reached: lack of roads, the nomads' characteristic wandering, and shortages of vehicles and workers in the south meant starvation. But all of this was easily dismissed. As the Harrarghe provincial medical officer, Ayele Kebebe, explained: "People have always starved down in the desert and help has never reached them before." Little help was reaching them in 1974.

In Margado, missionaries found thirty nomads starved to death, their water holes dried up, their cattle dead. The few survivors were eating *bure*, a yam-like root. The relief programs in the south, run by missionaries, were reaching only "a small fraction" of the starving. In Bale, one region of 90,000 people had 75,000 starving, and deaths were reported as "several hundreds per week." The Norwegian Lutheran Mission brought food and distributed it to 173,212 people in Gemu Gofa but reported to CRF: "This relief program is reaching only a small fraction of the area affected, which is approximately 110,000 square kilometers with a population of 1-1.5 million."

Even the total number of starving people in the south was unknown.

In the spring of 1974, UNICEF's program and planning officer, Stephen Green, who made the 1973 report, again pieced together information from missionaries, estimates from provincial authorities, and various Ministry of Agriculture surveys. He concluded: "It is our belief that the Government estimates of the number of drought-affected persons in the South is still quite low." Green said that in Kaffa, Gemu Gofa, Sidamo, Bale, and Harrarghe provinces there were "close to 2,000,000 persons needing food assistance, certainly through July and possibly through the end of the year. Of this number, fully 500,000 are in a 'famine' situation, as opposed to a food shortage situation."*

Green saw three options: these starving people would either, (a) get food in their villages, (b) mass in the market towns as in Wollo and Tigre a year earlier, or (c) starve. "The prospects for alternative (a) for many of the people," he reported, "look slimmer every day."

The United Nations Disaster Relief Organization (UNDRO), though an agency with little power, acted quickly in 1974, sending out an urgent message for food. The estimated requirement for grain had been increased in early 1974 to 164,000 metric tons to cover the spreading famine in the south. But by spring, less than 123,000 metric tons had even been *pledged*. No relief grain, for example, had reached Gemu Gofa Province at all by late March, 1974, where 160,000 people, according to the governor, were starving to death. In fact, by late spring, no famine relief had reached most parts of southern Ethiopia, despite Stephen Green's report. Relief workers began saying that the alarm had been rung too late again.

"It's all over," one of them told the *Washington Post*. "At this stage, given the beginning of the rains [making transportation difficult] and the size of the area, there is nothing we can do. Logistically, it can't be done.

"We've only seen pieces of the picture. But we know enough from a variety of reports to say that a Wollo-Tigre type of famine could occur over an area that is three times the size of these provinces and with twice the population."

Obviously, few people knew precisely how desperate life was in southern Ethiopia. One who did, however, was a tattered cattle herder in Harrarghe Province, who observed:

"We can no longer afford to buy grain by the bag. Now, we must buy it by the cup."

---

*By "famine situation" Green meant starving, as opposed to merely hungry.

Getting relief grain to the starving Ethiopians proved difficult. As the grain arrived at the three ports used by Ethiopia—Massawa, Asab, and Djibouti—red tape and bottlenecks delayed shipment inland. At one point, the Ethiopian government refused permission to use storage facilities, and relief grain rotted in the rain.

Strikes closed the three ports for up to a month. Massawa and Asab, both in Eritrea Province, are vital port cities. Massawa connects to Asmara by road and by 306 kilometers of narrow-gauge railroad. The port of Asab is reached by a highway from Addis, which passes through southern Wollo and the Danakil region. Ethiopia also uses the port of Djibouti, in the French-run Territory of the Afars and Issas, which connects to the Ethiopian cities of Dira Dawa and Addis Ababa by an 880-kilometer narrow-gauge railroad. All three ports were used for relief supplies, and ships carrying relief grain got priority berthing and off-loading.

But delays on the docks at these ports stopped grain from reaching the starving. Only Massawa in northern Eritrea, which supplied Tigrean and Eritrean relief centers, had few difficulties. Small amounts of corn-soy-milk from UNICEF were delayed, but Ras Mengasha Seyoum made sure trucks and drivers were available and cooperative. But at both Asab and Djibouti, relief grain and supplies began piling up on the docks in early 1974. In Asab, for example, an American embassy official found 2,300 tons of fertilizer, badly needed for planting new crops, and 5,000 metric tons of relief wheat stacked on the docks in January and not moving. He alerted Washington, but little could be done.

For one thing, the State Department kept shifting the arrival dates for grain shipments to Ethiopia. Ironically, most ships hauling grain from the United States in 1973-74 were heading for the Soviet Union and not the hungry nations of Africa. As a result of these changes, grain reached the Ethiopian ports at irregular intervals and with disastrous results. On May 12, 1974, some 13,500 metric tons arrived from the United States, followed by another 13,500 metric tons in early June. Other donors were also making deliveries, and without skilled dock workers to off-load the supplies, the grain piled up.

Moreover, the IEG, facing civil unrest and the threat of a coup, was immobilized. Donors asked Ethiopian officials for military vehicles and troops to clear the ports and were told that the vehicles were needed by soldiers, who were (in turn) needed to keep guard, especially in the southern provinces (watching Somalia) and in Eritrea. The irony was bitter; troops who could have moved grain were held back to keep an eye on people who were starving.*

Grain shipments inland dropped to a trickle. At Djibouti, there were 18,000 metric tons of relief grain waiting shipment to the provinces. Some of this was U.S. Public Law 480 food. The only means of transporting the grain was by railroad, and the railroad workers went on strike for an extended period of time. Furthermore, regular warehouse storage space was already full of grain, and relief supplies were stacked in the open where they began to rot. Moreover, one-third of the railroad freight-hauling cars owned by the Djibouti-Addis railroad were being used as *permanent* storage wagons (not for grain), parked on sidings in the Dira Dawa area. This created shortages of railway cars to move out the relief grain to Harrarghe, Wollo, and Shoa provinces or to haul exports to Djibouti.

Foreign aid officials demanded that the ports be cleared. But there was little coordination among the donors, and none within the IEG. Shipments of grain arrived haphazardly. Distribution inland was left to the whims of railroad workers and truck drivers. When Prime Minister Endalkachew Makonnen issued a directive ordering the railroads to provide wagons for relief grain shipments, his directive was ignored for four weeks. When the strike was finally settled, relief food moved slowly out of Djibouti. By July, 1974, eleven weeks after major shipments of relief grains began arriving, some 6,000 metric tons of food were still backlogged in Djibouti alone.

---

*At the end of 1974, some 700,000 Eritreans were starving.

Asab, dependent upon trucking, had its problems, too. Private truck drivers could have played a major role in the distribution of food and relief supplies. Some did. But just before the famine broke in 1973, Ethiopian truckers and the IEG argued over weights and fees. The IEG tried to muscle the National Transportation Company, an association of truckers with eight hundred lorries, to take a low rate, which they had refused, and bitterness remained.

Every year in Ethiopia, from November to May, there is heavy demand for trucking to haul export commodities to the ports of Massawa and Asab and to return to Addis Ababa with general cargo. Between November, 1973, and May, 1974, therefore, as the amount of urgently needed relief grain was pouring into Ethiopia in increasing tonnage, most of the country's trucks were busy hauling exports and general cargo. The transport of relief grain was unattractive to private turckers, largely because there were no back-haul loads from the drought areas of the north—let alone the desolate southern provinces—to Addis or the ports.

As a result, few trucks were available for carrying relief grain out of Asab. Moreover, in April, May, and June, when the railroad workers went out on strike, the dock workers and then the truckers followed. The flow of grain halted completely. Some 10,000 metric tons of relief grain piled up at Asab, as did other supplies. Relief agencies couldn't get anyone to transport blankets, for example, because only ten quintals of blankets could be fitted into a twenty-quintal truck, and the charge was made by weight, so haulage firms were reluctant to take them. Said one worker: "The children of Wollo need blankets, and I can't get them out of the port."

The port workers' and truckers' strikes made the famine situation critical. The Ethiopian government refused to release its own trucks—military, imperial highway, or police—to solve the problem and continued to insist on a low rate of pay for transportation of relief supplies, USAID's young emergency relief coordinator, Tom McClure, offered a special rate enhancement to the commercial truckers directly, bypassing the Ethiopian government, to carry relief grain rather than their normal cargo from the ports. USAID donated $200,000 to this, but there was only a slight improvement. USAID then asked that the Relief and Rehabilitation Commission fire the aged clearing and forwarding agent and hire a new one and also guarantee that a specific number of trucks be made available every day. USAID persisted and offered to "top off" truck rates as an incentive to drivers to haul the relief grain at $5 a metric ton. But however commendable the USAID initiative, the situation was incredible: Ethiopians were being paid bonuses to deliver food to starving Ethiopians.

By the end of May, exports had slowed, and trucks became available again. By early August, the backlog at Asab had dropped to 1,000 metric tons.

Once the grain reached the provinces, however, there were further obstacles to getting it to the starving. Before the seasonal rains in the south, for example, some 230 tons of grain donated by the European Economic Community had been flown in to an airstrip outside Arba Minch in Gemu Gofa Province. For several weeks this grain could have been picked up and moved to relief areas, where peasants were slowly starving to death without it. But, without any pressure from the central government, local administrators refused to cooperate and release the grain for shipment, and the police wouldn't haul it in their idle jeeps. With the rains, the grain started to rot, the bottom layer of sacks sinking into the mud.

With the exception of Tigre Province, moreover, few secondary roads exist in Ethiopia; in the south, only one tarmac road and many primitive tracks permit overland transportation during the dry seasons. Without such secondary roads reaching the provincial interiors, Ethiopia's people continued to suffer. Doctors reported that, within a day's journey by mule in the interior of Wollo, people were still starving to death by June, 1974; cholera and other diseases were killing the weak. One doctor who returned from a four-day trip into the interior reported finding fifty dead bodies in a single small village and the rest of the people lying about in various stages of death. Of the 170,000 peasants affected by the drought in the Negele Borana area of Sidamo Province, only 11,000 could be reached by relief teams. Bale lacked roads, and only 10,000 of the 160,000 in need could be reached.

Part of the problem was solved by turning to ancient forms of transportation: donkeys, mules, and camels. The International Red Cross in Wollo used camels to haul 700 tons of grain as far as 150 kilometers from storage points along the Addis-Asmara highway.

In some instances, helicopters were used. In late 1974, for example, helicopters hauled 500 tons of grain to interior missionary stations in the Konso district of Sidamo Province. They said that the villages were in very bad condition and the crops were destroyed by army worm.

Helicopters also had a drawback: Ethiopian officials liked to joyride in them. Legesse Bezu, the new governor-general of Wollo, commandeered an army helicopter for rides around his province. German helicopter pilots also had to chew out officials seeking free rides over Wollo and Tigre while doctors in the interior urgently needed full loads of supplies that could be brought in only by helicopter.

One day late in February, 1974, a young international relief worker hitched a necessary lift on a helicopter heading into northern Wollo. To his surprise, ten Ethiopian government officials scrambled on board. The helicopter was a heavy-duty French freight-carrying model needed desperately for hauling grain into the interior. But the Ethiopian officials had it diverted this day to hop them from town to town along the Addis-Asmara highway. At one of the stops, the relief worker cornered a representative from the Ministry of Commerce, Industry, and Tourism. Annoyed, he asked the Ethiopian: "What is your mission on this trip?"

Somewhat embarrassed, the ministry official replied that he was along to "find impediments to trade."

"Have you found any this morning?" asked the young man.

"Yes," said the IEG official. "Mountains."

Not surprising, Stanley Mitton, working in Ethiopia for the World Council of Churches, saw in Wollo "large stocks of grain at various places on the road, but apart from the efforts of individual expatriate missionaries there seems to be no overall organized effort to get the grain to the interior." And another relief worker in Addis Ababa wrote back to his agency: "Coping effectively with famine in Ethiopia is not a major priority among Ethiopian government officials, nor, I fear, is it the top priority for many of the foreign donors operating in the country."

It began to appear that the Endalkachew government wouldn't be any more effective against the famine in 1974 in the south than the Aklilu Habte Wold cabinet had been against the disaster in Wollo and Tigre in 1973. "Incredibly," one Ethiopian told the *New York Times*, "it looks like they are going to do the same thing this year that they did last year, which means that many people are going to starve."

June, 1974—*Report from the Field.*

> *Grain being distributed is only enough for a month, "and when that distribution ceases people will have nothing." Seed is provided to the farmers, but they eat the seed. In Lalibela, in Wollo, there are 60 quintals of seed but there are 6,000 people who want it.*

> *The Tigre Relief Committee (TRC) estimates it will need 680,000 quintals of grain through October, 1974, but has received only 88,107 quintals so far. TRC estimated that of 1.1 million oxen in Tigre before the drought, only 220,000 are left. People in Tigre "have become belligerent, making distribution difficult, sometimes impossible." There is "worsening need and hunger."*

> Feeding stations in Eritrea forced to close "because of the political situation." Workers gave 5,000 vaccinations for cholera "and reported perpetual famine around the Red Sea area." Two CONCERN* nurses in Adigat state that "the numbers of malnourished are increasing monthly." Typhus outbreak around Wegessa. Estimate that Danakils have lost 80 per cent of their cattle.
>
> "The problem is that wherever you go people are desperately poor and the difference between a famine victim and a poor person is very slight indeed."

July, 1974—*Report from the Field.*

> *In Maji* awraja *of Kaffa Province, one of the hardest hit districts in the south, "people depend upon roots and leaves for survival, which [have] little nutritional value."*

---

*CONCERN is a Dublin based relief organization.

Officials in Addis Ababa remained aloof from what was happening in the countryside. Except for the brief tour of Wollo in November, 1973, His Imperial Majesty remained in his palace, worried perhaps about the rebellion rising around him. The IEG couldn't prevent strikes in its port cities, let alone get relief food smoothly from dock to province or penetrate the interior where the supplies were needed most. Amid such incompetence, exploitation flourished. And where there was exploitation and indifference, there was also massive corruption.

While peasants died, some Ethiopians thrived. There were benefits for a few during the worst of the famine: land was sold by hungry peasants to wealthy landlords and village chiefs, often for as little as $2.50 an acre, when there were buyers. Not only did some Ethiopians buy these tracts of land—and thereby increase the concentration of land ownership, the greatest single political and social problem in Ethiopia—they also bought livestock and relief grains. These items were then resold on the commercial markets, sometimes at three times the original price, to relief groups. Grain speculation began, driving up prices. And those who paid the most were those who could afford it least: the missionaries and volunteer agencies battling starvation in the field.

This was the ultimate, bitter irony about the Ethiopian famine: unlike the Sahel, or any other starving nation in the world, Ethiopia always had available within its borders the resources for halting its terrible famine. Throughout 1973 and during the first half of 1974, while tens of thousands starved, other Ethiopians hoarded and exported grain.

Between March and September, 1973—the worst periods of the famine in Wollo and Tigre provinces—there were some 20,000-30,000 tons of grain stored in commercial warehouses around Ethiopia. These grains included teff, wheat, barley, maize, and sorghum. Those 20,000 or more tons were at least *half* the amount needed to keep all of the starving peasants of Wollo and Tigre alive throughout 1973. Had the IEG, the World Food Program, and the donor nations acted together—using these 20,000 (or more) tons of grain, plus emergency shipments of other food and supplies (perhaps airlifted in)—no famine would have occurred in Ethiopia in 1973.

The IEG, however, remained silent—demanded silence from others who knew—and chose not to use its own grain to feed its people.* Moreover, in April and May, 1974—long after the Ethiopians had asked for large amounts of grain from donor nations and while famine was spreading in the south—a USAID marketing survey revealed "an estimated commercial surplus" of about 30,000 tons of grain in dealers' warehouses. In addition to such commercial stocks, the National Grain Corporation (NGC) had in storage in May, 1974—and in 1975—about 17,000 tons of wheat. This wheat, purchased under a standard commercial agreement, was imported in 1971 from Australia. It remained securely in storage throughout the famine period.

Not until September, 1974, did the Ethiopian government declare a state of emergency in Wollo Province. By that time, grain speculation had made rich Ethiopians richer; Ethiopian and other traders pocketed windfalls from the famine and relief efforts. Said an international banker, who presumably would know: "A lot of personal fortunes are being made out of famine aid."

Relief workers in Wollo and Tigre seethed at the "considerable store of grain" held by landlords in those provinces. An American embassy officer in Ethiopia reported seeing "peasants starving to death within a few miles of grain storage." The Crown Prince, Asfa Wossen, had "bulging warehouses of grain" in Wollo which were held off the market while peasants starved. In May, 1974, a relief worker checking grain in the town of Makele in Tigre Province, found 187 tons in private storage. Local government officials denied that this was available for famine relief and, further, refused to allow police, government, or municipal vehicles to distribute it.

---

*During 1973, the IEG borrowed 7,000 metric tons of grain from its private stocks and later replaced it with U.S. government relief supplies.

Classic market fluctuations were played carefully. As long as large amounts of relief grain were held off the market or, preferably, not even brought into the country, shortages (and high prices) could occur and profits could be made. When the 1972-73 harvests generally failed, the price of food grains rose in perfect classical economic fashion. In some markets, prices shot up. The IEG's Ministry of Agriculture reported in mid-1973 that grain in Tigre was selling for $205 a ton, twice the normal price of $102 a ton. Major grain markets in Addis Ababa, Asmara, and Dessie reported 1973 grain prices up 33 per cent above the 1972 level. Sorghum prices in places like Jijiga, near Dira Dawa in Harrarghe Province, jumped from $5 per quintal to $20 per quintal during 1973.

There was little concern for the impact of this on the starving or on the missionaries and volunteers who tried to buy grain on the commercial market to feed them. Local officials near Bati, a hard-hit area, held relief grain off the market, slowly selling it as the price rose. The relief workers, without donated grain, had to pay the going rate. The Norwegian Lutheran Church bought food in the south for 90,000 people. The Norwegians also purchased more than 1,000 tons of food and seed grain from the local markets in Sidamo at high commercial prices and tried to feed 173,000 people. But the grain prices kept rising. "Soon," one worker reported to Christian Relief, "we will not be able to purchase any." In March, 1974, no relief grain was going into Sidamo and Gemu Gofa, and missionaries were still purchasing what grain they could find on the open market. "Precious funds are being wasted on high local grain prices," one complained, "while relief grain is available in the northeast parts of the country."

Obviously, a large influx of *free* grain would depress this rich market. Not only did the IEG not declare an emergency in 1973 nor publicly ask for massive aid—which would have brought the grain into Ethiopia quickly—but it also dribbled what relief grain it did have into the provinces. As mentioned, an IEG cabinet minister revealed privately that between April and August, 1973, only 1,400 metric tons of relief grain reached the starving people of Wollo and Tigre provinces—barely enough to feed 10,000 people where 500,000 were starving.

As prices rose, at one point the Ethiopian government offered to *sell* 4,000 metric tons of grain it had in storage to the United States, which could then *donate* it back for relief inside Ethiopia. In September, 1973, several Ethiopian Grain Corporation (EGC) officials approached a USAID staff member and asked him to divert incoming shipments of American relief grain—the May pledge—which the EGC officials hoped to export for sale to Yemen and Saudi Arabia where prices were high. They would then replace those shipments by purchasing grain on the

Ethiopian market after the December harvest when prices in Ethiopia are lower. The deal never went through because USAID refused to countenance it, but it is remarkable for its brazenness and insensitivity. Had it worked, the deal would have deprived starving Ethiopians of food and, at the same time, further inflated domestic grain prices being paid by, among others, the missionaries and relief volunteers.

Incoming relief grain was manipulated and held off the market by the IEG. The figures for 1973 are difficult to obtain and suspicious when examined. But in its November, 1973, report, the IEG claimed that it had received just 4,468.7 tons of grain from donor sources, *excluding* the 2,000 tons of Food-for-Work grain diverted in May by USAID and the 5,000 tons of in-country grain obtained from World Food Program. Together, this would have given the IEG 11,468.7 tons of donated grain during 1973.

But by its own accounting, the IEG claimed that it distributed in 1973 to the various provinces through its relief committee, *including* the 2,000 tons of U.S. and the 5,000 tons of WFP grain, the following amounts:

Wollo	3,185 tons
Tigre	1,124 tons
Shoa	790 tons
Gemu Gofa	245 tons
Harrarghe	220 tons
Red Sea area	203 tons
Begemidir	44 tons
Total:	5,811 tons

Taking the total amount the IEG claimed in its November report to have received in 1973—4,468.7 tons—and adding the 7,000 from the United States and WFP, the IEG had an undistributed surplus of 5,657 tons of relief grain.

What did they do with it? According to the Ministry of Agriculture, the IEG put some 982 metric tons of grain into the local markets "at a subsidized price." It held off another 982 metric tons of U.S. grain, stored at Asmara, for two months during the harvest period of the summer of 1973, claiming it was "not clean." During that time, prices rose, and the grain, clean or not, was distributed.

There were better markets than those frequented by starving peasants and desperate relief workers. And, by the second half of 1973, world grain prices had soared. A query to U.S. embassies in surrounding countries indicated that grain prices in Yemen, for example, were almost double those in Ethiopia. The temptations were strong.

Figures for the first quarter of 1973 showed that the export of pulses (peas, beans, and lentils) was up 92 per cent over 1972. The quarterly bulletin of the National Bank of Ethiopia concluded in its September, 1973, report, "It now appears that large stocks from the excellent 1972 harvest and adequate supplies in 1973 from the rest of the country are sufficient to satisfy current demand." In the middle of the worst of the drought and continuing until November—long after careful documentation of the extent of the food crisis—Ethiopian merchants exported hundreds of tons of grain, beans, and even milk to Western Europe and the Saudi Arabian peninsula. In 1973, while 100,000 of its people starved to death, Ethiopia exported 9,000 metric tons of grain—almost double its 1972 exports. That 9,000 metric tons would have fed most of those 100,000 people for about three months.

Not all the exported grain was grown in Ethiopia. The IEG, as mentioned, banned exports of cereals and oilseeds to all countries except the Territory of the Afars and Issas (Djibouti), traditionally dependent upon Ethiopia for its grain.* The Djibouti connection would prove lucrative.

Large quantities of Ethiopian grain travel the Franco-Ethiopian Railroad from Addis Ababa to Dira Dawa and into Djibouti for export. As mentioned, one-third of the railroad cars owned by the railroad were used for permanent storage. These could be manipulated easily. When relief grains started coming into Ethiopia from the donors, said one report, "a rather large quantity" of it got diverted. Some was shipped out of Djibouti in railroad cars that got reshuffled in Dira Dawa and returned to Djibouti for export. Other grain came in, got rebagged, shipped to Djibouti, and exported. That created another irony: of relief grains coming into Ethiopia passing rebagged relief grains going out.

The USAID Office of Inspections and Investigations documented in July, 1974, that at least 300 tons of relief corn and 1,000 tons of relief wheat had been rebagged, reshipped, and exported from Djibouti. French sources in Djibouti state that at least 1,800 metric tons of relief wheat alone had been rebagged and exported through Djibouti during the first six months of 1974, when large quantities of relief aid had started coming into Ethiopia.** By July, 1974, 100,000 metric tons of grain and

---

*Djibouti, a French colony, buys Ethiopian grain because shipping costs are cheaper. Grain-rich France, on the other hand, prefers to sell food to more lucrative European markets but sells arms to its penurious colonies.

**The Ethiopian government made a half-hearted investigation and stated on July 31, 1974, that "there has been no export of any type of grain from this coun-

4,234 tons of high-protein food had been delivered to Ethiopia's three ports. (It was still far below the 164,000 tons needed or the 122,300 tons pledged.) Even the *Ethiopian Herald* raised allegations about the rebagging.

What was documented as rebagged was a small fraction of what was suspected. Christian Relief (on August 26, 1974) reported that some of the relief grain coming into Ethiopia "cannot be accounted for" between the ports and the inland distribution centers. That was only the beginning. Christian Relief grew increasingly concerned about "where the grain went from these [distribution] points." Keeping track of relief grain required a major administrative effort—one which neither the Ethiopian Relief and Rehabilitation Commission nor Christian Relief nor the individual donors (as long as they refused to cooperate) could mount. Grain was pledged, arrived, and got trucked to distribution points. Where it went then—to the hungry or back to the ships for export—was anyone's guess. About the same time as the Christian Relief expressed its concern, USAID issued a report stating that it was unable to obtain "adequate records" of relief grain movements to the interior of Ethiopia. Inventory records at some warehouses, USAID found, "were less than complete."

In addition to exporting home-grown and rebagged relief grains, Ethiopia also exported other food supplies as well. Here again, food crops grown and stored within easy shipping distances of the starving never reached them. Instead, as Ethiopia was doubling her 1973 grain exports over those of 1972, the country was additionally exporting 177,000 tons of pulses. Further, oilseeds, exported despite an official IEG ban, raised the total for cereals and pulses to some 250,000 tons in 1973—a staggering amount of exports for a country whose people were begging for food and dying from starvation.

In an editorial on January 18, 1974, headed "Effects of Drought," the *Ethiopian Herald* bragged about the high prices obtained for haricot beans: "The good harvest this year was confined only to haricot beans. This agricultural product, which is not part of the Ethiopian diet, has had a very high demand on the international market and this has had very favorable results. It must be noted here that it was not the volume of export but the high price per unit which was to account for the returns from haricot beans."

---

try except for the Territory of the Afars and Issas. The Commission feels however that the authorities in Djibouti might have been misled by the acquisition by the Territory of the Afars and Issas of 1,327 tons of maize and 1,975 tons of wheat sent from Ethiopia, a practice that has been going on for some time." Despite the disclaimer, an Ethiopian television newscast on the evening of August 1, 1974, reported that the Relief and Rehabilitation Commission would prosecute two persons for illegal re-export of relief grain.

Here, once again, the international donors knew about the exports—news was carried in the *Herald* and in the quarterly reports of the National Bank of Ethiopia—and said nothing. Relief workers, however, paying high prices at the markets, pressed IEG officials about the exports. The official reply was that pulses were not normally eaten by the peasants, that hungry peasants would resist them, and that a change of diet would be dangerous to those suffering from malnutrition and weakened by famine. Relief workers, however, were quick to argue that starving people seldom reject food, even haricot beans. Further, the exported haricot beans would have been, for the Ethiopian famine victims, an excellent source of protein, and the oilseeds a good source of calories. Moreover, as an FAO report on food points out, an Ethiopian gets 85 per cent of his meager caloric intake from cereals, ensete, and pulses; and, "they [pulses] constitute a very important part of the diet."

But these were petty details. Whether or not a starving peasant will eat pulses or haricot beans was incidental to the fact that food supplies, and especially grain, were being exported from Ethiopia. No one spoke up, and the exports—including the rebagging of relief grain—continued through 1974.

In fact, it took a major confrontation between the Ethiopians and the international agencies to get anyone to speak out about what was happening. And even here, the protests came late and were lost beneath high-politics considerations on the Horn.

In October, 1974, Ato Shimelis Adugna, commissioner of the Relief and Rehabilitation Commission, issued a major alert: the drought and famine in Ethiopia covered eleven of the fourteen provinces and affected three million people. Ato Shimelis called for 278,000 metric tons of grain in 1975. "We know a crisis is around the corner," he said, "and I don't want to wait until it is here." At the same time, however, donors were growing skeptical. The harvests that fall had been good in Ethiopia, temporarily easing the tragedy. Some relief agencies were closing down their feeding stations in Wollo and Tigre. Others were turning to the drought and food crises in India, Pakistan, and Bangladesh. Further, drought in other parts of the world had reduced the amounts of food available, and it was unlikely that the international donors would give the 278,000 metric tons asked for by the Ethiopian government.

The controversy quickly turned to the ability of the Ethiopians to tap their own resources—both grain and money. In fact, in 1974, Ethiopia's grain exports were double those of 1973, which were double those of 1972. During the two years after the peasants' bold march on Addis, the Ethiopian government had received free more than 150,000 metric tons of grain from international agencies and donors, most of it arriving in 1974. But the Ethiopian government had purchased just 2,000 metric tons of grain from local commercial markets. It had refused to distribute 17,000 metric tons imported from Australia and held in local warehouses or to purchase any of the 30,000 metric tons of Ethiopian grain privately stockpiled during 1973-74. Further, it had quadrupled its grain *exports* during a time of mass starvation.

In addition to the 278,000 metric tons of grain asked for from the international community, Ato Shimelis wanted 60,000 metric tons for a national emergency stockpile. One reason for the high grain request, donors suspected, was that the proposed agrarian reform, if carried out, might cause further drops in agricultural production, and the central government wanted a large grain reserve to deal with possible rural discontent and food shortages.

The U.S. embassy sent off a request to Washington to reserve 20,000 metric tons of grain in case of an emergency in Ethiopia during 1975. But other donors, especially the international relief agencies, now spoke out freely. They pressed the new Military Council, in power since the arrest of Haile Selassie on September 12, 1974, to use its stocks of grain to feed its own people or to buy the undonated amounts on the world market. The conclusion reached by these donors was that the military leaders could purchase the grain needed to feed their people during 1975. "If you're going to have a revolution in Ethiopia," said one international banker in Addis Ababa, "this is the best time to do it as far as the financial picture is concerned." During the first quarter of 1975, Ethiopia held about $314 million in foreign cash reserves, or the equivalent of more than one year's foreign export earnings.

There were many demands on these cash reserves. For one thing, Ethiopia's petroleum bill may be three times higher in 1975 than in 1974. For another, the new Military Council, coincidental with the request for more donated grain, decided to step up the suppression of guerrillas in Eritrea Province. By January, 1975, Mengasha Desta, the minister of finance, had made plain to the U.S. State Department that Ethiopia would rely on all donors for her grain and, by implication, on the United States alone for her guns. To spend cash reserves on consumables would not, he argued, solve Ethiopia's long-term problems.

Eritrea was, by early 1975, one of Ethiopia's major political and military problems. Somalia was another. As documented, the United States had supplied extensive amounts of military equipment to Ethiopia since 1953. Between 1960 and 1974, moreover, Ethiopia got as much as 70 percent of all U.S. arms shipments to Africa. During the first week in February, 1975, as the fighting in Eritrea depleted stocks of Ethiopian weapons and ammunition,* the Military Council turned once again to

---

*The Ethiopian army faced Eritrean guerrillas that were better equipped: the Eritreans had Russian AK-47 rifles, Chinese plastic bombs, Soviet-made RPG-7

the United States. Ato Kifle Wodajo, recently Ethiopian ambassador to Washington and now the new foreign minister, met with Secretary of State Henry Kissinger and made his request for between $25 and $30 million worth of light arms and ammunition. The Military Council stated its willingness to buy the weapons with hard currency. The Ethiopian government, which by that time had been fighting in Eritrea for ten consecutive weeks, asked for an emergency U.S. airlift of the military equipment.

In fiscal year 1974, Ethiopia had purchased $22.3 million in weapons from the United States, half in grants and half in sales. In FY 1975, the United States promised another $11.3 million in grants and $11 million in credit sales—an identical amount. Also, Washington had approved in principle the sale of another $53 million worth of arms to Ethiopia for cash—which would bring the total arms package close to $100 million during 1974-75. Washington, increasingly dependent upon foreign arms sales to help with its own balance of payments, made its message clear to Addis Ababa: Take the rubber band off your foreign cash roll.*

Ethiopia's total budget is $362.5 million, of which she spends $50 million for military expenses. But of that $362.5 million, perhaps $255 million is her own money, and the rest is foreign assistance loans or grants. Therefore, Ethiopia is actually spending $50 million of her own $255 million—or 20 per cent—on military items. An economist at the American embassy in Addis commented: "That's very high by African standards. If you look at Africa, you find that the Sudan, Ethiopia, and Somalia are the high spenders on military equipment. That's because the Horn is the hot corner."

The high-politics of this hot corner obscured the fact that Ethiopia wanted guns and needed grain, but was only willing to pay for the guns. While the high-level policy planners in Washington and other world capitals weighed and the world press focused on the major issues—the arms buildup in Ethiopia; the Russian presence in Somalia; the strategic significance of the Bab el Mandeb Straits; Red Sea, Persian Gulf, Indian Ocean scenarios involving the Soviet Union, the United States, the Arab states, and Israel—Ethiopians starved.

It was clear in 1975 that Ethiopia needed a large commitment of

---

rocket launchers, and SAM-7 heat-seeking missiles, among other modern military equipment.

*Although Congress has imposed a $40 million limit on military loans and grants to all of Africa—of which Ethiopia gets by far the major portion—the current arms-selling trend is to phase out grant programs in favor of credits and straight sales. Credits, however, remain only a small percentage of all arms deals. Only 15 per cent of the $8.2 billion worth of arms bought worldwide in 1974 was purchased on credit. The remaining 85 per cent was purchased with cash.

arms and men to hold onto Eritrea; in early February, half its army occupied the province. But Eritrea was only part of the military's concern. To the south, there was the old rival, Somalia, well armed with new Russian weapons, including MIG-21 fighters. Adding to this, Tenneco and other consortiums were drilling in the Ogaden Desert (an area claimed by Somalia and occupied by Ethiopia). Natural gas has been discovered in small amounts in the Ogaden, and should oil be found in commercial quantities, Somalia (so went Ethiopian fears) might take advantage of Ethiopia's internal turmoil to strike across the desert and seize territory long considered part of Greater Somalia.

To hold Eritrea and to defend the Ogaden, the Military Council needed more ammunition and newer arms, and that could not be accomplished without U.S. military aid. At a late February, 1975, meeting of the Washington Special Action Group, chaired by Secretary Kissinger in his capacity as chairman of the National Security Council, and with representatives from the CIA, the Joint Chiefs of Staff, and the secretaries of state and defense, a basic decision was made: Ethiopia would get more U.S. arms. On March 17, the United States announced that it was selling to Ethiopia (on a cash-only basis) at least $7 million in emergency military equipment; most of this is small arms and ammunition to replace expended materiel. The Ethiopians, meanwhile, started serious weapons shopping: to Iran for F-5As and to private arms dealers for M-60 tanks, armored cars, and other heavy weaponry.

It appeared that Ethiopia, at least temporarily, would get both guns and grain.

The aftereffects of Ethiopia's drought and famine run deep and contain profound implications about her future. Ethiopia is a microcosm: by examining the lessons of her drought and coverups, we see the inability of traditional diplomacy to respond to new problems taking place; the increasing paralysis of the UN civil service because of pressure from member states; the inability of special agencies to respond to issues that are cyclical worldwide and, in fact, occurring even now.

We also learn from Ethiopia's experience the kinds of choices and demands that will be placed on the international community in the decades to come. For drought is not unique to Ethiopia, nor is starvation occurring only on the Horn. The long-term effects of the drought upon Ethiopia detail a grim portrait and carry special import and obligation for all of us.

Let's look at Ethiopia's future. In early 1975, the United States, among others, increased its drought relief to Ethiopia. The United States granted $4.3 million for emergency drought relief, bringing the American relief-and-rehabilitation grants to about $28.2 million since 1973, most of which was used to supply 67,000 metric tons of relief foods.

The new grant was earmarked for digging wells, resettling 35,000 nomads, and developing food crops. It was not unlike grants from Sweden, West Germany, Great Britain, China, and others. As well-meaning as these grants were, they overlooked a basic fact: the drought and famine that swept Ethiopia destroyed the country's physical ability to sustain itself at any time during the next decade and, without more fundamental steps, perhaps ever again. Shortages of plow oxen and seed may be overcome with aid—and should be. But conditions such as cyclical drought, overgrazing and erosion, widespread malnutrition and disease, and poor agricultural productivity dictate Ethiopia's continuing dependence upon the goodwill and concern of others for at least the rest of the century.

First—crop and livestock losses. Sixty per cent of the nation's crops have been destroyed, most of them in the traditional food supply areas. The chances of a full harvest during 1975 appear slim: the Christian Relief Fund estimated at the end of 1974 that Ethiopia's farmers needed $1.2 million worth of plow oxen and $1.8 million worth of seed. USAID stated that 80 per cent of Ethiopia's cattle had died in 1973-74, half her sheep, and 30 per cent of her goats and camels. The Ethiopian Livestock and Meat Board stated in 1974 that the effects on the people in the drought areas would be "long-range since sufficient recovery of livestock numbers cannot be expected for 3-5 years." The UNDP, too, was pessimistic with a report at the end of the year that not only were livestock losses heavy, but also new stocks would be extremely difficult to maintain. "Over wide areas the grass is gone," said the UNDP, "and it will take many years to re-establish. Indeed, there are places where a grass cover may *never* revive under natural conditions." (Italics added.)

Trees have also gone with the grass. And, while the Military Council buys $100 million worth of arms, Ethiopia is—literally—going down the river. Erosion washes away the finest agricultural soil in the country. As previously cited, the IEG's report in November, 1973, called the impact of the drought "unprecedented" and stated that its "causes may go beyond the mere fact of the failure of rains to come at their usual time and in their usual quantity. . . ."

"What alarmed the nation in . . . 1973," said the Ethiopian government, "was not merely the magnitude of the problem. . . . Throughout Tigre and good parts of Wollo, and elsewhere the ecological balance has been seriously disturbed. . . ." The provinces most severely affected were those with the longest history of agriculture. "Long settlement has meant progressive de-forestation and soil erosion. While the capacity of the soil to produce and sustain human and livestock existence has been severely curtailed the human and livestock population has grown—and grown rapidly in recent years."

Overpopulation and overgrazing opened up slopes that shouldn't have been cultivated, which reduced yields and increased erosion. Fifty years ago, the Ethiopian highlands were covered with trees. Today, they are barren. If the erosion isn't halted immediately and more than 100 million trees planted, whoever finally wins in Ethiopia, loses. The countryside won't be able to feed a population that even today is malnourished. As the Ethiopian government warned in its November, 1973, report:

"Among the first and foremost steps that should be taken to prevent a further deterioration of the ecological balance and to build up resources wherever this is practical and possible is afforestation. The immensity of this problem is evident to anyone that has seen the denuded countryside of Wollo and Tigre. It is inadmisible to give up hope or reduce the scale of the effort required on that pretext. Existing afforestation programmes in the two provinces need to be intensified and expanded substantially."

Ethiopia's immediate, short-term agricultural needs are massive amounts of seeds, plow oxen, and reforestation, among others. While some programs are going along on a small scale, the need is widespread. Further, agricultural planning in Ethiopia is at a standstill, awaiting completion and (most important) implementation of the new land reform program.

Second—health problems. The Ethiopian peasant-farmer needs extensive health care to recover from the drought. Throughout Ethiopia, the majority of the people are malnourished, weak, susceptible to disease—and, worst of all, highly vulnerable to another drought. They are, in the words of one USAID official, "living on the razor edge of existence."

That means that an Ethiopian child in the famine provinces now dies in a few days from simple measles, or an adult dies in a few months from TB. In Wollo, for example, Dr. Tamerate Retta, a young Ethiopian who returned from his studies in France to help combat the effects of famine, said that the urgent need in 1975 is for post-famine medical care, especially for the children. The U.S. Public Health Center for Disease Control in Atlanta, Georgia, together with UNICEF, surveyed the south and concluded: "There remains great vulnerability among large segments of the population to malnourishment and the contraction of potentially lethal diseases such as tuberculosis and measles." With the new drought and famine, vulnerability means death.

An additional cause of poor health in Ethiopia is lack of clean water. Fewer than 3 per cent of her people now drink uncontaminated water, and many Ethiopians suffer from water-borne intestinal diseases. One diplomat in Addis stated: "The best medical instrument in Ethiopia is a spade—to bury human excrement and dig wells."

During the long drought of 1970-74, death from thirst came frequently and was, observed one missionary, "an even more terrible death than from hunger." At the Serdo camp along the Addis-Asmara highway, twenty-four people died in one week from thirst. Within Wollo and Tigre, the Imperial Highway Authority owned perhaps thirty-eight water storage tanks, and twenty were in excellent condition with water in them. They were never used. While all relief camps, and most of the provinces, suffered from lack of water, the district of Awsa, covering one-third of Wollo, was "one of the worst hit areas." There was no water, no food. The governor allocated a 1,000-gallon tanker, and one came from the Americans at Kagnew Station, "but it was not in good condition." In July, 1974, it was "still standing idle until spare parts can be acquired to put it into operation."

The few clean-water wells in Ethiopia are badly over-used. There are 30 people to a water well in the United States, 66 to a well in Sweden, and 50,000 to a well in Ethiopia. In normal periods of good rainfall, many Ethiopians must spend up to six hours a day fetching water. Even then, there's no guarantee that the water isn't contaminated. As one African official emphasized: "If we can't get clean water, there is little point talking about food."

Another persistent health problem among the Ethiopian people is malnutrition. The average daily intake of calories is just 2,020, which is almost 10 per cent below the requirement for maintaining health. The obvious way to prevent people from being weakened by malnutrition, and thus susceptible to disease, is to raise their caloric intake—feed them more. But to increase the nutritional standard of the Ethiopian people to a level of health—that is, above malnutrition—would require an agricultural output increase of between 30 and 40 per cent.

Third—resettlement problems. The outlook for Ethiopia's agricultural growth is grim. Without agrarian reform and a major overhaul of the entire agricultural system, which will be difficult to carry out successfully without outside assistance, the country's output will not increase beyond its present meager offerings. It is moribund. The levels of farming technology are low, the land tenure system is incentive-killing, the methods of storage and marketing inadequate, and the cost of transportation prohibitive. And the outlook is pessimistic.

The most important first step toward increasing agricultural output, getting the peasants at the feeding stations back to their land, has proven to be a difficult task. For example, in 1974, as in 1973, the Ethiopian government and the relief workers tried to get those who could to leave the shelters and return to their villages to plant. By May, 1,400 people had left the shelter at Dessie, and 297 had left the shelter at Kermissie to return to their home *awrajas.* So strict was the government's order that, even after 1,483 people had left the shelter at Kombolcha to return to their villages, those remaining outside were not admitted "unless suffering from gross malnutrition or malnutrition with associated disease." The camp at Bati was surrounded by people who, because of the governor-general's order not to expand the camp and to get the people out to their villages, had been refused admittance. They lived, ate, slept, and defecated around the camp perimeter. One missionary reported: "In a very short time, with the increase of the hot weather, there is no doubt that the most appalling epidemics will occur unless some vigorous action is taken."

The Ethiopian government, with major help from USAID, planned to supply needed draft oxen and seed and set up seventy food distribution centers in the interior of Wollo and Tigre provinces to feed the people between harvests. The plan was put together in 1973—and nothing was ever done. In fact, in Wollo alone, the total program called for providing 12,500 oxen. By June, 1974, more than 30,000 farmers had signed up, but none of the promised 12,500 plow oxen had arrived. And not only did the number of farmers far exceed the number of plow oxen, but any oxen for sale on local markets cost 200 per cent more in 1974 than in 1973.

Without plow oxen or seed and with their land suffering from the effects of the drought, the Ethiopian farmers couldn't regenerate their farmsteads. Food supplies ran out, and the trek back to the shelters started all over again in June, 1974—the harvest season. The inflow was first felt at Dessie, perhaps because peasants were also shifting from other shelters that tried to close. Dessie's camp population, during the first six months of 1974, had dropped from 5,000 to a few hundred. It jumped back to 5,200 by the end of June, and Oxfam hurriedly erected 3,000 tents to shelter the overflow; there was food for only 2,400. The number increased to 6,000 by September, 1974. Elsewhere, Kobbo took in 746 residents, with another 427 living outside in what CRC workers said were "very bad conditions."

Clearly, famine relief had created a feeding operation that the Ethiopian peasant came to depend upon. Free food, Ethiopian government officials argued, encouraged the peasants to expect the government to feed them, or know the reasons why not. Obviously, there is social and political danger in creating such dependency: a peasant class expecting food during times of shortage, and not getting it, becomes a base for rebellion. Moreover, if the peasants don't return to their villages and farm their land, agricultural development cannot take place. The military government has been strict about closing shelters in the drought areas, even at a cost of causing additional hardship, rather than allowing the peasants to become too dependent.

Cynicism among the well-fed in Addis and other towns became

popular. Even some donors argued that too much grain had been made too readily available and that the peasants had come to depend upon it. Some peasants, these officials claimed, were adopting a life of "comfort" at the relief shelters—a bit of an overstatement given conditions there. Commented one comfortable Ethiopian in Addis: "The only thing these people are dying from now is laziness." The long-term prospects of their dying from starvation, however, are better.

Four—the need for agricultural reform. Drought and famine may well be cyclical in the Horn, and Ethiopia's remaining feeding shelters may expect a continuous ebb and flow of peasants. Even during good times, most small farmers in Ethiopia live at the edge of starvation before each harvest. One reason is that—until agrarian reform really is able to change things—each peasant farms too little land: in Tigre, it is one hectare per farmer. The nationwide average is 1.5 hectares per farm holding, and that may include four or five noncontinguous plots.

According to a 1974 FAO report concerning Ethiopia's long-term ability to grow her own food, the present small-plot, peasant-farmer system is incapable of raising agricultural output without also increasing the area cultivated. That is, with the sowing of crops limited by oxen-drawn wooden plows and harvesting done largely by hand, peasants cannot increase food output on their small plots. Any output increase is only proportionate to increase in the size of the farmed plot.

Basically, this means that without successful agrarian reform and imaginative agricultural programs, Ethiopia will increasingly be unable to feed itself. Moreover, the dependence on small peasant plots, the population pressure on arable land, reduced fallow periods, and progressive erosion, FAO reported, make it "likely that yields will *decrease.*" (Italics added.)

Aid projects in Ethiopia are too little, and perhaps too late, to alter this. Agricultural schemes are being run by USAID, the Swedes, and the British. USAID and WFP also operate a Food-for-Work road-building program in Wollo, and there are well-drilling, irrigation, resettlement, and housing projects. The World Bank is plunging $10 million into resettlement projects, reforestation, health facilities, and feeder roads. Even the Military Council allocated $63.3 million for relief and rehabilitation work through September, 1975, the largest amount ever marked for such use by the Ethiopians. Both Christian Relief and Ato Shimelis Adugna's Relief and Rehabilitation Commission have turned from feeding programs toward special aid projects.

But most aid programs, including USAID's much-heralded Minimum Package Program (MPP), are located along the major roads, not in the interior villages where most of the people live (and starve). These programs also encourage inadequate small-scale farming—to do otherwise is too sensitive politically. Even so, USAID and FAO project that the MPP will produce an additional 412,000 tons of cereals by 1985. It won't be enough.

The FAO report, with thorough documentation from a World Bank Agricultural Sector Survey and the U.S. Appraisal Report of the Minimum Package Program, provides a realistic assessment of Ethiopia's agriculture. The prospects of increasing the output of food crops in Ethiopia are gloomy. The outlook to 1985, FAO reports, "is not satisfactory"; and, despite USAID's hopeful MPP, there will be by 1985 a cereal *deficit* of nearly 150,000 metric tons every year. "Even this projection," said FAO, "may be unrealistically optimistic as it assumes a 2.1 per cent annual increase in food crop production outside the MPP programme."

The FAO outlook raises another question: Are the proceeds from any successful Ethiopian harvests enough to prevent repeated starvation? The answer is no. Already, demand for food is outstripping the country's ability to supply.

The demand for cereals constitutes two-thirds of the total calories in the Ethiopian diet. This is estimated in 1975 to be increasing at precisely the same rate as the rural population growth. Those who are not farmers—the market-dependent population, the urban Ethiopians with their higher incomes—consume more food and food grains. And *their* population will double by 1985. Their consumption of wheat, mostly in the form of bread, will triple by 1985. Already, in 1975, according to FAO, rural wheat production lags behind wheat consumption in the urban areas.

"It must be accepted," said the FAO, "that for several years the country will be barely self-sufficient in good seasons, and will be very vulnerable to droughts." But the prime agricultural areas are already experiencing irregular and often inadequate rainfall and disastrous erosion. Moreover, what crops survive are attacked by army worms; in 1974, 40,000 square kilometers in Harrarghe and Sidamo were defoliated by these insects,* which destroyed much of the maize and sorghum crops. According to the FAO report, such natural calamities, joined by

---

*The Military Council had only 150 tons of insecticides to spray on the army worms, and the Ministry of Agriculture got stocks of 100 per cent DDT from the Malaria Eradication Program in Addis, 20 tons from a private company, 20 tons of 100 per cent DDT from Kenya, and 22 tons of 100 per cent DDT from FAO. USAID supplied 150 hand sprayers. "The side effects of DDT are well known," cautioned Christian Relief, "but [the Ministry of Agriculture] feels that it is worth risking the lives of a few people to save thousands."

the inaccessibility of many farming districts and the lack of reserve stocks of grain, "make these large areas of Ethiopia very vulnerable to famine conditions."

Even if Ethiopia's food production can gear up and increase, as FAO reports, at the "unrealistically optimistic" rate of 2.1 per cent per year, it won't feed her people. Ethiopia's population is growing at 2.5 per cent per year and will reach thirty-four million by 1985. Even now, emergency food distribution has to continue during "good harvest times."

FAO suggests that to feed one million Ethiopians for a year will take 150,000 metric tons of relief grain at a cost of at least $20 million. (The cost will increase, of course, if droughts strike food-producing regions on other continents.) But there are, according to FAO, already two million Ethiopians "completely destitute." So $40 million a year would simply sustain life (such as it is) in rural Ethiopia. To raise the caloric intake to levels above constant malnutrition, to improve health, to create large-scale, long-term development schemes, to stimulate both agricultural and industrial growth might, according to the U.S. State Department, cost $1 billion a year and require fifteen years for this single nation (admittedly a state of twenty-six million people and one of the largest of the developing African nations).

Ethiopia's immediate needs—plow oxen, seeds, reforestation, improved health—must be met in order to give any hope to her long-term requirements. Because of her location on the Horn, her central role in African and her important role in world politics, and the publicity given her drought, famine, and coup, much is known about Ethiopia and her problems. A microcosm of past disaster, Ethiopia could become a study of hope.

The very international agencies—starting with the United Nations—that covered up Ethiopia's plight in 1973 should now pool their expertise and power to attack those long-term problems. There are historic precedents of nations helping one another with massive aid during short-term national disasters. But what about long-term and massive aid?

During the drought-famine in 1974, the aid that poured into Ethiopia was overwhelming: whole prefabricated field hospitals, huge feeding programs, airlifts of volunteers that, for too brief a time, made a change and offered hope. A similar program, coordinated through the new Ethiopian government and using Ethiopians (or training them) in positions of policy- and decision-making, should now be undertaken.

The basic point is that new thinking about how aid policy is made and who gets affected by it must commence by the international agencies, which are now too remote and politically paralyzed. Is it excessive to hope that by focusing the attention of these agencies, by massive long-range planning, by selling (or giving) Ethiopia the needed goods and programs over several decades, by offering expert technical volunteers (doctors, agricultural specialists) the country could be turned around? What does it mean for the future of that important section of Africa and for relations between the developing and developed worlds if it is not?

The alternative to this massive, deliberate, and international commitment is intolerable. Put together, Ethiopia's erosion, persistent ill-health, malnutrition, agricultural needs, food demands, and deficits lead to two conclusions: large and dependable inputs of foreign aid, or prolonged periods of widescale rural starvation.

Famine in the Horn is not an event of the past, but of the future: it is cyclical. By September, 1975, drought and famine were sweeping southern Ethiopia again, affecting perhaps one million people; at least 70,000 had entered fourteen relief camps by summer, 1975. It was also spreading into Somalia, Kenya, and Tanzania. At one camp, Kebri Dehar, there were 14,000 starving and sick people and two nurses. "I was in Wollo during the drought there," said one eyewitness, "and I would say what's happening in the Ogaden is much worse."

The short rains failed in the south for the third successive year. What meager grazing the Ogaden offers dried up. Nomads began entering the towns searching for food. In one region of Harrarghe, Dagahabur, some 108,000 of the 300,000 people faced starvation, according to the assistant administrator of the region. In one town, 75,000 people lived on dried milk and corn supplied by the Military Council and distributed by the Ethiopian army. Father Kevin Doheny of CRF visited the area and found water so scarce it was being sold.

This time, the Ethiopian government publicly asked for aid. More than thirty-four countries had responded to Ethiopia's plight with aid in cash and kind that exceeded $70 million.* But there were continuing disputes among the international agencies over how much aid Ethiopia

---

*The United States had contributed more than $18 million and 60,000 metric tons of relief grain.

really needed. For by the time of the long rains in March, 1975, 200,000 Ethiopians again depended upon relief aid in the Ogaden area alone.

By 1975, it was clear that Ethiopia's "problem of drought" had become a regional crisis of people. To the west, 50,000 nomads in the Bahr el Gazal Province of the Sudan were affected by drought. In the Ogaden, the Shibeli River, which normally floods and irrigates the isolated pockets of arable land on its course through Somalia to the Indian Ocean, had failed to flood. Somalia, which depends upon the Shibeli for water, suffered. Drought made half her arable lands temporarily sterile.

By June, 1975, some 4,000 Somalis had starved to death, and 250,000 Somali refugees were crowding into twelve relief camps. The United Nations appealed for relief supplies and food, but officials warned that the situation "was deteriorating rapidly and required much more outside aid than had been estimated." Ibrahim Megag Samater, economic advisor to Somalia's President Muhamed Siad Barre, told a news conference at the United Nations that 800,000 people—25 per cent of Somalia's population—might require relief aid.

Kenya was also suffering. In 1974, 70 per cent of her countryside and two million Kenyans were affected by drought. In the Turkana and Marsabit districts, on both sides of Lake Rudolph, and the Northeast Province, 60 per cent of the population needed outside assistance in 1974 to prevent widespread famine. The Kajiado District along the Tanzanian border, populated by Masai, lost perhaps 100,000 head of cattle from drought. In both the Machakos and Kitui districts, crop failures in 1974 reached 80 and 100 per cent. Kenya began importing wheat to meet her demand.

In Tanzania, the *ujamaa* program was in deep trouble: 3,000,000 people had been moved—some willingly, some not—to communal farms. Farm production fell: early plantings in 1974 dried up or washed away; the winter wheat crop around the main growing area east of Arusha was one-third normal in March, 1974, and 50 per cent normal in August. The maize and rice crops were also half normal. In May, 1974, the American ambassador, without delay, declared an emergency and made $25,000 available for "humanitarian requirements."

But by December, Tanzania was balanced on the edge of disaster. It had to import 40 per cent of its food in 1974 and had gone begging to the world market for food aid, with limited success. The United States provided 20,000 tons of grain as a grant and 40,000 more on easy credit. But the United States also turned down a Tanzanian request for 200,000 tons of corn, the national staple, on the grounds that the United States had none to spare. President Julius Nyerere, pushing the *ujamaa* communes hard, told his people: "Our motto must be: 'Produce or perish.'" The results will come in 1975, and if the rains are not heavy, Tanzania, too, faces the spectre of widespread starvation. "We have no money and we have exhausted our foreign reserves," President Nyerere said. "If we do not have adequate rains we will be faced with serious famine in which people will die."

Despite the lessons of Ethiopia, both Tanzania and Kenya have tried to keep the coverage of their droughts quiet. (Only the Somalis, faced with an extreme and perhaps uncontrollable situation, have called early for aid.) The general secretary of the National Christian Council of Kenya, warned in a letter asking for "any assistance you can give": "The Government [of Kenya] does not want publicity given to the situation and we therefore request you to proceed very discreetly. Although the drought situation is severe enough, the Government are [sic] nevertheless raising local foodstuffs to meet the major part of the famine relief required."

Kenya's approach is to use relief groups already in the country who are, said one worker, "under no circumstances to generate any publicity about the needs or about their relief work." The National Christian Council and the Kenyan government set up thirteen famine relief camps and donated food. But the government of Jomo Kenyatta, already shaky and perhaps worried by the overthrow of Africa's other leading elder to the north, made it clear to National Christian Council leaders that it did not wish in any way to be "embarrassed over the issue" of famine. Offically, the drought situation is under control in Kenya, and there is a local news freeze on the subject.

The coverup of a national crisis is not unique to famine, nor to Africa. But basic changes have taken and are taking place in international diplomacy; new issues are arising primarily in the economic field, and their more prominent place on the international agenda should be reflected in the attention top policy-makers give them. Another Ethiopian crisis does not have to occur again and again elsewhere—and yet it may.

In 1959, when 100,000 peasants starved to death in Ethiopia, few agencies and fewer nations offered to help. The indifference of the developed and developing nations permeated the decision-making levels of government. International political considerations dealt with global war, not regional starvation. But by February, 1973, when the Ethiopian peasants made their desperate march, the ugly fact of global starvation had begun to shake the comfortable assumptions of the international community. Perhaps for the first time, the well-fed became directly connected to the hungry: by the electronic press; by shortages at home; by rising prices and the diminution of tangible comforts; and, most frightening, by the *threat* of global catastrophe and future personal discomfort.

Ethiopia, in 1973, became an example of problems facing the

international agencies on a global basis. These agencies and the donor nation administrators shared their unwillingness to sacrifice political considerations, in retrospect very short range, for humanitarian concerns of more enduring importance. In fact, the famine in Ethiopia shows us that those men and women whose job it is to handle drought and food emergencies or publicize outbreaks of disease are unwilling or unable to do so. The technical problem of discovering, measuring, and warning about a cholera outbreak should be a routine, apolitical task, like measuring rainfall. The United Nations, however, as it has become more and more cautious in the face of pressures from interested member states, is permitting these technical tasks to be distorted. Now, international agencies must wait for approval of governments before making even the simple announcement that people are dying in some country. In Ethiopia, thousands of helpless peasants were sacrificed for this attitude.

The politics of starvation in Ethiopia—and today in other countries—had many silent partners. The OAU met in Addis Ababa during the height of the famine and remained silent. Why? Its members, and the members of the diplomatic community in Addis, whispered about what was happening in the countryside, but no one spoke out, including the African nations, silent when their Ethiopian brothers needed them most.

There were ways to break this silence. One wonders what the effect might have been—both inside Ethiopia and out—had the major embassies passed the word in May, 1973, that they were giving up the cocktail parties and diplomatic dinners because of conditions that existed in Wollo and Tigre; or couldn't the international community have called attention to the drought in a way that would have minimized the embarrassment to Haile Selassie? When a hurricane strikes Honduras, the people there do not blame the government for the disaster. The storm is seen as an unavoidable catastrophe, and help sought from all sources. Could not the bureaucrats in the United Nations, reading the reports from the field, have concluded that a widespread disaster had occurred in Ethiopia and the Horn and announced it as a regional crisis? Selassie could have gone to his people with the statement that the United Nations had called Ethiopia's famine an unprecendented disaster and that aid was available. But silence was easier, and it allowed old relationships to continue.

It was, finally, these coveted relationships that blocked aid reaching the starving Ethiopians sooner. And these relationships are still a vital part of national and international bureaucracies. It is important to realize that those who "blew the whistle" on the coverups first, and longest, were the lower-echelon diplomats, including the Ethiopians themselves. Those who sat on information, who remained indifferent even as peasants marched on the capital, who abetted the coverup were the older civil servants and foreign service officers who had built up working relationships and contacts they refused to jeopardize.

Beyond this, while the less senior men and women were shocked by and issued warnings about the "low-politics" event of mass starvation, their superiors continued being concerned with "high-politics issues: the security of the Selassie government (badly misjudged, as it turned out); the strategic and political issues of the Horn, etc. These highly visible (and important) political and military issues obscured a basic humanitarian fact: people were starving to death and nothing was being done.

One could argue that the drought and famine coverup was the fault of the older diplomats—of Haile Selassie, of Ambassador Ross Adair and other ambassadors in Addis at the time, of the older Ethiopian or international civil servants. But this is too easy an assessment: it was not the fault of age, but of a fundamental system of normal diplomacy. It was the *normal* patterns of diplomacy—the traditional way of doing things—that allowed a well-reported famine to be covered up. Further, it was the traditional, normal diplomacy that didn't—or couldn't—react to an extraordinary event like widescale starvation.

Normal diplomacy places the highest premium on stable and friendly relations with the host government. Everything is subordinated to that goal. Warnings from the field—eyewitness reports—then had to be ignored to preserve normal working relationships.

Here, in its worst sense, is a continuing public policy generation gap. Low-level bureaucrats often find that their first assignments are in the low-politics fields, like economics and aid. Ironically, in an age of economic interdependence, their field is becoming increasingly important; yet one wonders whether the changes in the international system are that evident to an older generation of civil servants trained in a different environment.

Further down the line, we learn from Ethiopia, are those people in the field—in the case of the drought, missionaries. The evidence of the crisis was always there in the notes and observations of these missionaries who, in frequent cases, were the only people to visit certain areas—and still are. Yet few talked to them, and those who did—workers like UNICEF officials or two young anonymous State Department contacts—learned fast of the horror spreading across the countryside. But apparently there is no effort by senior officers in international agencies, senior diplomats, or—far worse—journalists to consult such people regularly. The official word for governments, international organizations, and the world media still is: No crisis exists until those appointed to announce a crisis do so.

These traditional patterns of behavior must be reevaluated and changed. One bitter relief worker in Ethiopia complained: "Unfortunately, the central priority of many public and private expatriate donors is the development and preservation of the harmonious relationship with the host government rather than taking the necessary and often politically sensitive steps of getting the relief job done. Consequently, for many expatriate donors, on an operations level, *a disaster does not occur until the host government officially says it occurs.*" So it happened in Ethiopia.

This raises a final, basic point, that of national sovereignty. When do humanitarian concerns override national (or international) political issues? In the approaching era of possible resource scarcity, as other Ethiopias elsewhere may unfold their disasters, honoring every fine prerogative of national sovereignty against all logic and evidence when catastrophes sweep whole regions becomes absurd. Indeed, the problems facing several nations in the future are likely to be so unprecedented that the idea of national sovereignty in the context of national automony will become an empty shell. Yet today's diplomatic practices call for respecting that shell, regardless of the consequences of events occurring inside that country.

One major benefit of this study should be to stimulate a search for new ways for outsiders to help nations facing internal economic difficulties without risking embarrassment to the local government. A major educational effort should be made to establish that it is not a mark of local government failure to be the victim of natural disasters like the one which struck Ethiopia. Nor is it a mark of shame in such circumstances to turn to the international community for assistance. Here the UN secretary general could play a more positive role by using his office to support debate of these matters. Now perhaps is the time for a call for a major survey of the effects of the drought on the African countries affected in the Horn, with a view to specifying corrective measures, on a regional basis with international assistance, which need to be taken.

The specialized agencies could help by reasserting their professionalism—their ultimate protection—and refusing to accord individual member states a veto over such questions as whether a cholera epidemic is announced. Foreign assistance agencies in developed countries could contribute to reform by developing and perfecting joint contingency plans for cooperation in crises like Ethiopia's and by encouraging the international media to pay more attention to evolving international humanitarian issues.

Breaking through an official coverup and national pride, however, will be difficult. India, for example, faces serious food shortages. Amid growing criticism of the New Delhi government—and the silence of food officials—bleak reports reach the capital of widespread hunger in five of her twenty-two states. Smallpox and trachoma thrive, and blindness caused by malnutrition strikes thousands of children. In Bihar alone, 60,000 people, mostly children, suffer blindness from small pox that killed 20,000. "The food situation has become desperate," states an India weekly. "The management of the food economy is in a shambles."

About this time, an American in Washington, D.C., chats with a high-ranking official in India's embassy. Toward the end of their conversation, the American comments: "I'm sorrry about the famine in India, and I hope our aid helps."

"Famine?" asks the Indian official. "What famine?"

AFTERWORD

By Stephen J. Green

Perhaps the most serious crime that a government can commit, short of a campaign of genocide against its own people, is consciously to ignore the existence of a major disaster, or knowingly to deny the needed relief to its people when such an emergency occurs. For the result, as we saw in Ethiopia in 1973, may be the random death and suffering of hundreds of thousands of those least able to protect themselves—the children, the aged, the sick and infirm.

And yet, for this most serious of crimes, there is no international remedy, nor even any means of calling attention to it. The Hague and the Geneva traditions of international law, by contrast, provide numerous protections for the human rights of individuals caught in conflicts between states, or even in civil wars within states. If a conquering power razes the houses of civilians in occupied territories, the International Committee of the Red Cross (ICRC) can intercede under the Fourth Geneva Convention. Other conventions provide protection for the wounded and sick, for medical personnel and chaplains, and for prisoners of war.

True, the ICRC can only be effective in its interventions if the governments concerned allow it access to those whose human rights are at risk. Nevertheless, the Geneva Conventions bind signatory states by law to provide that access. And failure to abide by the Conventions can bring down upon the head of a regime several kinds of international pressures.

But there is no haven in international humanitarian law for the person whose government consciously ignores or even contributes to the gradual starvation of his children, or to their death by disease, when that government has the power to prevent the starvation and disease. Short of the overthrow of the offending government, short of a violent revolution by the disaster victims, no remedy exists, for the international community has no present legal means to intervene and prevent or mitigate the human effects of such criminal behavior.

In the light of the experience of the last three years in Ethiopia, the extention of international law into the field of natural disasters would seem to make the most obvious common sense. Several hundred thousand persons died.* The international community poured tens of millions of dollars into a horribly inefficient relief operation, too late to save the lives of most of those who needed that relief. Endemic cholera certainly spread further into neighboring Kenya, Somalia and the Sudan. And the criminally negligent regime of Haile Selassie was destroyed anyway, in spite of (perhaps, in part, because of) the efforts of good diplomats and international officials to spare it embarrassment. Civil war broke out openly, and the feudal state of Ethiopia began to disintegrate.

Hardly the results expected or intended by the diplomats. And yet, even the very officials who lived through the Ethiopian famine are, like most of the rest of their peers, skeptical of the utility and feasibility of international agreements which might prevent similar occurances in the future. Why? Because they believe (and hope, to some extent) that sovereign national governments will never approve arrangements for international intervention which would put limitations on their own national sovereignty even when necessary in natural disasters.

In order to understand why many officials resist such proposed international agreements, one must appreciate the perspective, the posture of most of those who pursue careers in national foreign services and in the United Nations.

Upon their arrival in Addis Ababa, for example, foreign mission heads and UN agency representatives presented their credentials to Emperor Haile Selassie, or to his representative. Centuries of tradition were symbolized in this act—the diplomat or agency representative concerned acknowledging the legitimacy of the regime, and the regime (in return) recognizing the individual as the official representative of his

---

*Though the final numbers vary, the Relief and Rehabilitation Commission of the Ethiopian government, the Ethiopian Parliament, UNICEF, the Christian Relief Committee and numerous press sources have all issued estimates in excess of 200,000, and some considerably over that figure.

country or organization, authorized to undertake the traditional activities of the embassy or office concerned. It is this ceremony which admits an ambassador or UN agency representative to a select club.

It was not the people of Ethiopia who accredited the officials when they arrived in that country, nor was it the government of Ethiopia in any enduring conceptual sense. Rather, it was the regime, in the person of the Emperor. This is an important distinction, for it helps explain why the U.S. ambassador, the UNDP resident representative, the UNICEF area representative, and virtually all of the many other officials in Addis were so ready, later, to accept the regime's cover-up of the famine. There were no famine victims present at the accreditation ceremonies of these officials. There were no peasants—only representatives of the regime in power.

There is, of course, another view of modern diplomacy which argues that a diplomatic mission, in protecting the long-run interests of its government in a foreign country, must look beyond the regime to the underlying social and political realities which will shape the future destiny of the country. This second view does not deny that the fundamental immediate task of a diplomatic mission is to conduct diplomatic business with the regime in power, but it believes that a mission fails if it stops there.

In Ethiopia, a few "junior" diplomats and international civil servants did attempt to respond to this minority view and pressed their colleagues to take action before it was too late. Hopefully, one result of Jack Shepherd's account of the mistakes made in Ethiopia will be to encourage a similar response by diplomats and international civil servants, particularly at the senior level, in future crises. But it is important that we be realistic. We must expect that most ambassadors and UN representatives will continue to adhere to the traditional concept of diplomatic responsibilities. These men and women will contend that they are in a foreign country to forward the more immediate interests of their own governments or organizations in that country. Accomplishing this means working smoothly with the regime in power.

Of course, hardly a day passes that these good people do not invoke the concepts of peace (the diplomatic corps), children and youth (the UNICEF representatives), public health (the WHO representative), etc. And these officials indeed work for such causes in an abstract, long-term form. The problem in Ethiopia in 1973 was that many people did not have any long-term interests. They were dying.

That they were dying was, somewhat curiously, perceived as a political embarrassment to Haile Selassie's government by that government and by virtually all of the foreign officials in that country. So nothing was done. This is the "bottom line" Senator Kennedy was searching for as he questioned the USAID official about why the U.S. government chose not to act, not to "blow the whistle" when action would have prevented starvation, but might have embarrassed Haile Selassie.

The terrifying thing is that, from this standpoint, in Ethiopia in 1973 the failure was not that of the prevailing view of diplomacy. It, and the officials who adhered to it, worked perfectly to serve the interests it and they were supposed to serve. One need not, therefore, be surprised by the lack of action, the lack of candor, which characterized the service of foreign embassies in Addis Ababa in the early, nervous, political stages of the famine. Rather one must marvel, in a perverse sense, at the skill and discretion with which the various ambassadors and international civil servants succeeded, for over eight months, in "protecting" the Ethiopian government by hiding the deaths of tens of thousands of Ethiopians from the rest of the world. In "protecting" it of course, they hastened its destruction (in the sense that the inevitable revelation of the coverup was perhaps the principal event triggering the military revolt).

We must, however, hold UN officials to a higher standard of honesty. For while they may operate as part of the diplomatic community, they are bound by the UN Charter. Article 100 of the Charter states:

> In the performance of their duties the UN staff shall not seek or receive instructions from any government or from any other authority external to the Organization. They shall refrain from any action which might reflect on their position as international officials responsible only to the Organization.

The UNDP resident representative, and the representatives of WHO, UNICEF, FAO and perhaps several other UN organizations did not only violate this article of the Charter, in Ethiopia in 1973, but also (in Mark Twain's words) they "flung it down upon the ground and danced upon it." And the headquarters of these organizations, as Jack Shepherd's manuscript amply documents, participated knowingly in the act.

Article 100 of the Charter also requires each UN Member State to "respect the exclusively international character of the responsibilities of the (UN) staff and not to seek to influence them in the discharge of their responsibilities."

There can be little doubt about the fact that Haile Selassie's government violated the letter and intent of this article. Is it not ironic that the one who evoked so clearly and effectively, in the 1930's, the concept of internationalism, should have spent the last few months of his reign desecrating that concept?

So long as normal diplomatic practice prevails, then, the major decisions in international disaster situations will likely remain squarely in the hands of the politicians who run the disaster-affected country. They will be the ones answering such question as:

- Do we have a disaster or not?
- Do we request assistance from international sources? Which sources?
- What types and amounts of assistance are needed?
- What arrangements are to be made for receipt and distribution?
- Should the relief be distributed so as to achieve ulterior political or developmental goals, other than the obvious ones of saving lives and restoring the status quo?

Under normal circumstances, of course, the prime responsibility for dealing with emergencies obviously rests with the national government concerned. But the Ethiopian famine of 1973-75 provides some grotesque examples of the price paid by disaster-affected populations, and the international community as a whole, when decisions are made by frightened, insecure, traumatized regimes. Several hundred thousands died of starvation and disease because a "government" was loath to admit the existence of a problem the publicizing of which might have adversely affected the tourism and agricultural exports which were the source of 70 per cent of the country's foreign currency reserves.

Clearly, there should be an international fail-safe system which can be activated when a government cannot or will not act, for the fiasco in Ethiopia was not unique, or even unusual. Recently, the "acknowledgement problem" occurred again in famines in India and in Haiti.* The price is heavy for this form of national sovereignty: In spite of all the resources and organizations involved, in spite of all the good will, the international disaster relief system is a non-system.

Unfortunately, many regimes react principally to the (perceived) political aspects of disasters, often ignoring the human effects. Early warning systems then short circuit. Governments and the international agencies look the other way. Private relief organizations begin to do what they can, with limited resources. The international press gets wind of the delay and/or coverup, and this becomes greater news than mere starvation and disease. The situation becomes dramatized, politicized. Defensively, the affected government and the UN agencies begin to act. Assistance goes into the pipeline and arrives . . . too late. Ill prepared,

---

*See *New York Times*, June 9, 1974 (Haiti); August 30, September 3 and 5, 1974 (India).

still defensive and struggling to deal with a sudden, modern logistics exercise, the affected government bungles the receipt and distribution of relief goods. The already negative press turns more sour. Long-term reconstruction and rehabilitation projects are hatched in an atmosphere which is thoroughly politicized, virtually poisoned.

This was and is the "scenario" in Ethiopia, and in an ever-increasing percentage of major international disaster situations. And it is totally unnecessary.

Why should the international community not share, from the outset, the responsibility and burden of dealing with a *major* disaster situation? Most major disasters *are* international problems—demonstrably so. In Ethiopia, WHO officials admitted that carriers of the cholera vibrios were probably crossing into nearby countries. When the extent of the food shortage was known, it was immediately apparent that large grain shipments from foreign sources would be necessary, even if existing internal supplies were effectively utilized.

With respect to food, and indeed all international relief inputs, decisions regarding priorities had to be made. Resources are scarce, and "international" disaster (i.e., those requiring some form of international assistance) are now occuring, according to the United Nations Disaster Relief Office, at the rate of one every three weeks. Ethiopia, or any other country cannot, should not presume exclusive access to the limited sources for international disaster relief.

Nor should the apportionment of those resources among emergencies be made, as they are now, on the basis of the amount of newsspace and number of tearful photographs which the international press chooses to devote to a given emergency. This is, precisely, the international disaster relief non-system: charity-based, demeaning to the recipient governments, and inevitably a wasteful use of donors' resources.

There is a growing concensus in international disaster relief circles that a series of international agreements are required, if order is to be made of the present confusion.

First, a way must be found to de-dramatize the initial, "discovery" phase following many sudden natural disasters, and most slow-developing ones. The political implications for the affected government must be softened, and international, professional assessments of the extent of damage in human terms and the specific amounts and types of relief needed must be facilitated.

Second, effective international mechanisms must be developed to deal with a series of specific technical problem areas that often derail major relief operations, such as food shortage and communicable disease early warning systems, customs duties on relief goods, telecommunications from the disaster area, and standardization of relief supplies and equipment.

Third, international relief operations simply must be better coordinated than they are now. The Red Cross, the church groups, the UN agencies, government relief assistance agencies and others should know, on a day-to-day basis, what each is doing. Even more important, coordinative mechanisms should be developed to ensure joint decision-making (with the affected government) among the various relief agencies in the field, in the disaster area itself.

If we are to deal effectively with these various problem areas, if the non-system is to become a system, a variety of international forums must be utilized. I have some specific suggestions:

Governments must agree in principle that major international disasters, like wars, *are* international problems, the resolution of which is essentially an international responsibility.

Over the last century, a growing tradition of international humanitarian law has sought to limit the scope and ferocity of war, at least in regard to its effect upon non-combattants—the wounded, the prisoners, and civilians in or near a war zone. This Geneva tradition of international law is founded upon the concept that human beings have fundamental rights that transcend those granted them (and often revoked) as citizens of a particular country.

The highest and strongest expression of this tradition is formalized in the four Geneva Conventions of 1949. To date, 135 nations have signed the Conventions, which now form a kind of irreducible minimum of constitutional law for each of these signatory countries in the sense that no regime or government can legally renounce these laws or rescind its commitment to be bound by them.

In a sense, too, the Conventions represent commitments regarding behavior in time of conflict which we have made to each other as individual human beings, over and above the uniforms we wear and the governments we serve. Many consider the Conventions to be the highest expression of our civilization.

In recent years the Geneva tradition has been extended in practice, though not in law, well beyond protection in wartime, to protection of political detainees in situations of internal strife within a country. This body of laws would seem to be an excellent framework, then, within which to guarantee, in principle, the human rights of disaster victims. A diplomatic conference involving, perhaps, a new Geneva Convention is a long-term effort, one which might require lengthy negotiations. Nevertheless, I think this would be the only way in which such agreements could be secured.

The idea is not a new one. In 1921 the International Conference of the Red Cross, composed of representatives of both governments and national Red Cross societies, put the matter concisely in a resolution calling for "the conclusion of a new Convention tending to a wider recognition of the Red Cross, of its peacetime role, and especially of its function in regard to relief for disaster-stricken populations."

In 1924, the Board of Governors of the League of Red Cross Societies raised the matter again in a resolution which expressed a wish for "the Geneva Convention to be completed by a Convention to establish the recognition, by Governments, of the Red Cross relief action in time of peace."

In 1929, the idea of an intergovernmental agreement on international responsibilities in natural disasters was brought up again in connection with the creation, in that year, of the International Relief Union. Like much of the rest of the paraphernalia of the League of Nations, however, the union was stillborn.

What I am proposing then, is the resuscitation of an old idea, the need for which has long been recognized. The experience with the hidden cholera epidemic in the Republic of Guinea in 1969 and the 1973 Ethiopian famine and famines last year in India and Haiti provide ample justification for this proposal. Such relief as the international community can provide to disaster victims should be mobilized quickly and effectively, and the initiation of this process should not depend upon a government's estimate of the effect of a "public" disaster upon its foreign currency reserves. Access to life-giving disaster relief should be regarded as a basic human right.

In a time of aggressive, defensive nationalism, many governments may resist this idea. And yet ironically, as subsequent events in Ethiopia have demonstrated, it is almost invariably the long-term best interest of a regime to face a disaster's human effects immediately, when they occur. International involvement at an early stage can help to deflect criticisms about delay or mishandling by one government. Recognition of the international nature of a major disaster is the best way to de-dramatize, to de-politicize the situation.

There is another advantage to the adoption of a new Convention, along the lines suggested above. The existing 1949 Geneva Conventions provide a role in law in conflict situations for the International Committee of the Red Cross (ICRC), as the preserver of the principles embodied in the Conventions and as the institution charged with the primary responsibility for application of these principles. From its founding in 1863 until the Second World War, the ICRC had gradually assumed humanitarian roles based upon its usefulness (to the parties of a conflict) as a uniquely neutral organization. The Geneva Conventions of 1949, however, formally recognized its role in law. The prestige, the substance of the ICRC was thereby greatly enhanced, and since 1949, the organization has extended its protection activities into a variety of fields not officially mandated to it by international agreement.

True, the unique position of the ICRC in international relations is based upon tradition and custom, the concept of Swiss neutrality, the expertize of its staff and a number of other factors, in addition to the 1949 Conventions. Nevertheless, it was the latter which made the ICRC something more than a private organization, and which has enhanced its official status.

By contrast, the League of Red Cross Societies, which is the federation of all national Red Cross societies and the agency which coordinates the activities of the International Red Cross in natural disasters, has no such substance, no such prestige. In official circles, the League is simply a "non-governmental organization." In practice, the League is only as effective as the member national society in a disaster-affected country. That local society must initiate and channel all League inputs in a disaster situation. As the national Red Cross societies are all auxiliary to the governments of the countries in which they exist, that initiation may not and often does not take place.

What I am suggesting is that the logical organization to discharge "international" responsibilities in disaster situations is the League. It should be given a role (fact-finding, the right of initiative, etc.) in disaster situations analogous to the role played by the ICRC in conflict siutations, as set forth in the 1949 Conventions.

Though there is not space here to discuss specifically what that role might be, I would suggest that the League might be given authority to determine, one would hope with the assistance of the affected country, but *without* the assistance if necessary, whether or not a disaster has occurred and what the human effects of the disaster are. If a national Red Cross society were under pressure from its government not to declare an emergency, the League could request the government to allow international inspection teams to visit the disaster area. Failure to admit the teams would constitute violation of the new Convention. The League would then be empowered to issue a report on the basis of the best information available.

The second type of international accord needed is technical agreements on specific, operational subjects, such as food shortage early warning, and relief operations telecommunications. The UN technical agencies would seem to be the best aegis for sponsoring and preparing the international conferences which might establish the uniform reporting requirements (for *all* countries), customs treaties, standardized broadcast frequencies and other technical accords which could so greatly facilitate the efficient operation of large international relief operations. Let us hope that the information sharing, expense and compromise involved in such understandings would be viewed by national governments as necessary costs in obtaining an improved international disaster relief system, which in turn would benefit donor and disaster-affected countries alike.

The final type of international agreement required concerns the arrangements for operational coordination of international disaster relief efforts.

There are presently two focal points for international disaster relief, both in Geneva: The League of Red Cross Societies and the United Nations Disaster Relief Office (UNDRO). The League chairs two coordinating committees in Geneva, of the organizations involved in disaster relief. There is a smaller group of five of the major agencies in the field, which meets informally, exchanging reports and generally keeping each organization aware of the known dimensions of each important disaster, and what each of the five is doing, on a more or less daily basis. In addition, the League hosts a larger monthly "round-up" meeting of representatives of twenty to thirty church and other private agencies, as well as the major UN agencies.

In 1972 a second focal point was created to coordinate the emergency programs of the various UN agencies, and to assist and inform government aid agencies which wished to participate in one way or another in disaster relief operations. General Assembly Resolution 2816 mandated these roles to the Office of the United Nations Disaster Relief Coordinator which has been laboring with mixed success since that time to bring order to the chaotic picture described earlier.

Several basic problems, other than the usually cited ones of limited staff and time, have prevented these two "focal points" from fulfilling their intended roles. First, the two organizations barely talk to each other at the working levels. They exchange cables and information notes, to be sure, and they occasionally even attend each other's meetings, but there is little operational coordination (such as arriving at a common estimate of the number of syringes needed immediately in disaster-affected country X, and then pooling funds and transport resources to meet that need).

Second, both UNDRO and the League are fairly frequently unable to act in a disaster situation, because both organizations are part of the system of traditional diplomacy. Effectively, both must await a government announcement of a disaster, before they can launch a major relief operation.

Third, and perhaps most important, neither the League nor UNDRO has a direct chain of command down to the field level. The League must work *very* discreetly through the concerned National Red Cross society, which may or may not be effective. UNDRO must hope that its "agent" in the field—the UNDP resident representative—attaches the same importance to emergency work which it does, and will take an active role in local coordination of relief operations. As the experience in Ethiopia indicated, these two arrangements amount to sub-non-systems within the overall non-system.

Personnel changes should go a long way toward solving the first problem, for recent disaster operations have sensitized many in the field to the need for cooperation between the League and UNDRO. A strong, independent League with a role in law could, as I have suggested earlier, solve the second. It is in the area of in-country operational coordination, however, that additional international agreements are needed. Ideally, the government of the affected country should play the directing/coordinating role for all foreign agencies involved in relief work. But experience has shown that where this does not happen, there must nevertheless be a focal point for coordination of the receipt of relief goods, and the internal transport, distribution, reporting and other activities of agencies with operations in the field.

The General Assembly might be the proper forum for clarifying such reponsibilities. Resolution 2816 could be amended to specify the role that the UNDP resident representative should play in coordinating the in-country relief operations of the various international and private agencies involved.

While the Red Cross movement in general, and the League in particular, as purely humanitarian organizations, are probably best equipped to deal with the delicate political aspects of disaster situations, the UNDP resident representative, with UNDRO and a raft of technical agencies behind him, is probably best prepared to fill a stop-gap coordinating role for the foreign agencies, should the government concerned be unable or unwilling to do so.

Perhaps the most effective way to ensure that such coordination occurs after a disaster is through the mechanism of pre-disaster planning. Disaster preparedness is one of those subjects like the weather, that everyone seems to talk about, but little is done about. It is incredible that in 1975, no systematic effort has yet been made by UNDRO or by the League (or preferably, by both together) to inventory existing national emergency plans in disaster-prone countries, select those countries where the plans are weakest, and then concentrate disaster preparedness assistance in those areas where it is most needed.

Where disasters occur frequently, this kind of assistance should probably be part of the national development plan itself, and thus should be included in the UNDP Country Programme. Existing UNDRO and Red Cross activities in this field are a patchwork quilt, and certainly not based upon a global assessment of needs. UNDP has to date virtually ignored the whole subject of disaster preparedness in its development assistance activities.

In my opinion, dealing effectively with major disaster situations requires that the international community begin to deal directly with these and the other questions raised above. There are, of course, very problematic judgment decisions that must be made here. When is a disaster properly a matter of international concern? When 50 people have died needlessly? Or 500? Or when 50,000 die? Who determines whether something might have been done to save them, or whether the government of the disaster-affected country has truly tried to deal with the matter on its own? It will not be easy to develop the international machinery to adjudicate these matters fairly and convincingly.

But surely when, as in Ethiopia, several hundred thousand men, women and children have succumbed to starvation and disease while their leaders watched and frolicked, somebody has violated the terms of his leasehold on "national sovereignty." And, realistically, the existing system of traditional diplomacy provides no answers. New mechanisms must be found to permit the international community to intercede effectively in such cases, and save lives.

Major human disasters are international problems, and they require international action. In 1975 the Ethiopian people would, I think, agree.

SELECTED BIBLIOGRAPHY

INTERVIEWS

In preparing *The Politics of Starvation*, I interviewed more than 150 people in the United States, Europe and East Africa. Much of the information contained in this report comes first-hand from these people or from reports they gave me.

Because the material is often confidential, because the subject is sensitive, and because these people work for governments, international relief agencies, the United Nations and other organizations, I have had to protect their identities.

A special thanks must go to these brave men and women who chose to speak up. They still work inside the United States State Department, the United States embassy in Addis Ababa, the Foreign Ministry of the Ethiopian government, the World Bank, the United States Aid for International Development, the U.N. Food and Agricultural Organization, UNICEF, World Health Organization, World Food Programme, the Church World Service, the Ethiopian Supreme Court, the Ministry of Agriculture of the Ethiopian government, the government of Kenya, the government of Israel, and several embassies in Addis Ababa.

NEWSPAPERS

Newspaper coverage of the drought and cover-up began with Jonathan Dimbleby's "Faint Hope and Charity" in the March 20, 1974, issue of the *Guardian* and with *New York Times* articles in February and March, 1974, by Charles Mohr. David Ottaway and Ronald Koven covered the story for the *Washington Post*. In addition, the London *Times*, the *Financial Times*, the *Observer*, the *East Africa Standard*, and the *Christian Science Monitor* also ran articles which proved useful.

The following is a selected list of the articles used in preparing this report.

Buxton, James. "The Threat of War in Eritrea." *Financial Times*, Jan. 3, 1975.

Dimbleby, Jonathan. "Faint Hope and Charity." *Guardian Extra*, Mar. 20, 1974, p. 16.

"Drought in Somalia is Said to Kill 1,500." *New York Times*, Jan. 30, 1975.

"Ethiopia Says Famine Was Covered Up." *New York Times*, Nov. 18, 1973.

Guillebaud, Jean-Claude. "Acid Test of the Revolution." *Guardian*, Jan. 11, 1975.

Johnson, Thomas. "Ethiopia, Battling Secessionists, Asks U.S. for Airlift of Arms." *New York Times*, Feb. 18, 1975, p. 10.

Knipe, Michael. "100,000 Estimated to Have Died in Worst Famine Since 1916." *Times* (London), Nov. 16, 1974, p. III.

Legum, Colin. "The Night They 'Hanged' Selassie." *Observer*, Sept. 15, 1974.

Linscott, Gillian. "200,000 Face Starvation in Ethiopia." *Guardian*, Nov. 14, 1974, p. 2.

Meredith, Martin. "Famine Leaves Rich Richer." Originally published in *Sunday Times* (London), reprinted in *Montreal Star News and Review*, Dec. 1, 1973.

Mohr, Charles. "Ethiopian Famine Hits Millions." *New York Times*, Feb. 15, 1974, pp. 1 & 8.

_____. "Ethiopian Famine is Still Spreading." *New York Times*, Mar. 23, 1974.

_____. "Hungry Ethiopia Said to Sell Food." *New York Times*, Feb. 24, 1974.

_____. "Rift in Ethiopian Society May be Deepened By Famine." *New York Times*, Feb. 18, 1974, p. 2.

Ottaway, David. "Belatedly, Ethiopia Begins Famine Relief." *Washington Post*, Sept. 9, 1974.

_____. "Drought Spreading in Africa." *Washington Post*, Apr. 7, 1974.

_____. "Ethiopia, Relief Units Differ Over Drought." *Washington Post*, Oct. 24, 1974, p. A18.

_____. "Famine Spreads in Ethiopia." *Washington Post*, Mar. 20, 1974, p. A1.

"Ousted Addis Government Blamed for Drought Toll." *East African Standard*, Aug. 28, 1974.

Willey, David. "One in Five Died in Ethiopian Province." *Observer*, Apr. 7, 1974.

PERIODICALS AND PAMPHLETS

"Ethiopia—End of an Era." *Africa Digest*, Oct. 1974, pp. 83-4.

"Foreign Interest in Eritrea." *Foreign Report*, Feb. 12, 1975, p. 6.

Griggs, Lee. "*Ujamaa's* Bitter Harvest." *Time*, Jan. 27, 1975, p. 45.

"Internal Economic Conditions: Ethiopia." *Africa Research Bulletin, Economic Financial and Technical Series* (Jan.-Feb. 1975): 3386 and (Oct.-Nov. 1974): 3290-1.

"Internal Security: Ethiopia." *Africa Research Bulletin, Political, Social and Cultural Series* (Dec. 1974): 3461-3 and (Nov. 1974): 3433.

"The Military Balance, 1971-72." *International Institute for Strategic Studies*, London. (The 1973-74 edition is also useful.)

Morris, Roger and Hal Sheets. *Disaster in the Desert*. Washington, D.C.: Carnegie Endowment for International Peace, 1974.

Oudes, Bruce. "The Lion of Judah and the Lambs of Washington." *Africa Report*, May 1971, pp. 21-3.

Stockholm International Peace Research Institute. "Arms Trade with the Third World." New York: Humanities Press, 1971.

UNITED STATES GOVERNMENT DOCUMENTS

U.S., Aid for International Development, Office of Eastern and Southern African Affairs of the Africa Bureau. *Summary of United States Government Assistance to Ethiopia*, prepared by Frederick Machmer, Aug. 2, 1974.

U.S., Aid for International Development, Office of Inspections and Investigations. *Ethiopia—Famine Relief Program, Re-export of Grain, Special Inquiry*, I.S.S. Case Report, June 16, 1974.

U.S., Congress, Senate. Subcommittee on Health of the Committee on Labor and Public Welfare and Subcommittee to Investigate Problems Connected with Refugees and Escapees. *Hearings on World Hunger, Health and Refugee Problems, Part IV: Famine in Africa*, 93rd Cong., 1st session, Mar. 21, 1974.

U.S., Congress, Senate. Subcommittee on U.S. Security Agreements and Commitments Abroad of the Committee on Foreign Relations *Hearings, Vol. II, Part 8, Ethiopia*, 91st Cong., 2nd session, June 1, 1970.

U.S., Department of State. *Area Handbook for Ethiopia*, prepared by I. Kaplan. Washington, D.C., 1971.

U.S., Department of State, Office of Media Services, Bureau of Public Affairs. *Drought Damage and Famine in Sub-Sahara Africa*, Special Report #10, undated.

UNPUBLISHED REPORTS AND MEMORANDA

Australian Freedom from Hunger Campaign. "Report of the Executive Director," AUSTCARE/AFFHC, Perth, Australia, 1973.

Christian Relief Committee. "First Report from the Christian Relief Committee to Relief and Rehabilitation Commission," Sept. 3, 1974.

Christian Relief Committee. "Minutes of the Meeting of the Ad Hoc Committee of the Christian (Emergency) Relief Fund" (in 1974 the name was changed to Christian Relief Committee), Addis Ababa, May-Dec. 1973 and Jan.-Sept. 1974.

Ethiopian Ministry of Agriculture. "The Drought Problem in Ethiopia," Addis Ababa, Nov. 1973.

Ethiopian Ministry of Agriculture. "Rehabilitation Activities in Drought-Stricken Areas of Ethiopia, Progress Report No. 5," Aug. 6, 1974.

Green, Stephen. "Chronology of the Non-Development of a Cholera Outbreak in Ethiopia, July and August 1973," memorandum to UNICEF, Aug. 14, 1973.

_____. "Information Package on the Drought Situation in South Ethiopia," confidential UNICEF memorandum to Francis Smithwick, Mar. 15, 1974.

Holmberg, Johan and Nils-Inge Albinsson. "Report on Visit to Wollo Province, 24-28 March 1974," Ethiopian Ministry of Agriculture, Mar. 29, 1974.

Mitton, Stanley. "Ethiopia Report—19 Dec. 1973 to 5 Jan. 1974," memorandum to Graeme Jackson. World Council of Churches, Geneva, Jan. 9, 1974.

U.N. Development Programme. "A Review of Implications of the Drought in the Stricken Areas of Tigre and Wollo Provinces in Ethiopia," Office of the Regional Representative, Addis Ababa, Oct. 2, 1973.

U.N. Food and Agriculture Organization. "A Policy and Plan for Improving Food Security in Ethiopia," Rome, July 1974.

U.S., Aid for International Development. "Status Report on the Ethiopian Drought," prepared by J. Shepard and G. Walker, Addis Ababa, July 7, 1974.

van Egmond, Alan. "Report on the Most Recent Famine Situation in Ethiopia," memorandum to Jan van Hoogstraten (Director of the Africa Department). Church World Service, New York, July 1, 1974.

World Council of Churches. "Contributions to Drought Relief and Rehabilitation Programme in Ethiopia as of 4 March 1974," Mar. 1974.

PRESS RELEASES

"Drought in Ethiopia." Press release by the Executive Board of UNICEF, Ref. #E/ICEF/L. 1292/Add .1, May 6, 1974.

"Sen. Kennedy Urges Emergency Food Aid for Ethiopia." Press release from the office of Senator Edward M. Kennedy, Nov. 27, 1973.